Wealth in the 21ˢᵗ Century

Wealth in the 21st Century

Drew Millett

Writers Club Press

San Jose New York Lincoln Shanghai

Wealth in the 21st Century

Writers Club Press
an imprint of iUniverse.com, Inc.

For information address:
iUniverse.com, Inc.
5220 S 16th, Ste. 200
Lincoln, NE 68512
www.iuniverse.com

ISBN: 0-595-14704-6

Printed in the United States of America

Contents

Introduction

Historians may look back and view the late 20th century and early 21st as a period of dramatic transformation in the standing of world powers. Many seemingly divergent events have occurred during this period of time. New technologies revolving around communication have altered the economic landscape. The collapse of the Soviet Union and emergence of China, both communist powers, could change what is understood as the best political economic system for the 21st century. At the end of the 20th century the United States could claim to be number one. Yet, changing world circumstances will impact America too.

Wealth in the 21st Century discusses the rise and decline of leading powers and the implications for the 21st century. Different nations have led at different times in history influencing world politics, economies and culture. Although there is a waxing and waning of national power, leaders emerge at particular periods of history. These cultures transform the thinking of a disproportionate number of societies changing the course of history.

The different cultures of the world have an order that can be understood and defined. Some have more influence than others. During the second half of the 20th century the world was organized into the First, Second and Third Worlds. With the collapse of the Soviet Union and its satellites the United States took lead role with Japan and Europe alongside. Surprisingly, some formerly poor nations began to advance into the ranks of the wealthy. South Korea, Singapore and China are examples.

Why do nations stratify into different levels of affluence? Shared geography and history influence the thinking of people. Over time, differences in the ability to survive differentiate wealth from one region to another. Eventually, one region develops greater influence and power in relation to others. Sometimes abundant resources are the key to success. The United States possessed natural resources (e.g. timber, iron ore and land) and developed a large continental market. Yet, historically, this has not always been a major factor. Japan is an example of a nation with few natural resources that has joined the wealthiest of nations.

An interesting comparison in the development of cultures is between the Americas and the Old World. Cultures from the Old World developed the wheel far before cultures in the Americas. Both regions would eventually have use for the wheel. Yet, circumstances in the Old World encouraged thinking that led these people to develop the wheel first. Geographical differences and their impact on survival appear to have played a crucial role in the development not only of the wheel but agriculture and other cultural artifacts.

How do some nations advance and come to dominate over others? Economic wealth is central to advancing a nation to the role of leading power. Other factors are important such as political, social and cultural influences. However, all of these depend on economic wealth for success. Some nations can rely on other means for a while. However, eventually, economic weakness undermines other areas of society. The Soviet Union is an example of a nation that increasingly relied on a non-economic area (e.g. military) to compensate for a weak economy. Yet, the Soviet Union's weaknesses soon became apparent as its society imploded.

Economic wealth is created when an ability to master the environment is created through technology. The wheel, mechanization of agriculture and development of new materials such as steel increase the amount of wealth generated by a population. More material goods are created with the same number of people. This technological breakthrough ripples throughout society generating other breakthroughs in technology. Synergy is achieved. Eventually, other countries learn to copy the leading nation's techniques and surpass it with another technological breakthrough.

Religious, political and cultural beliefs change as a result of technological change. Different areas in society are interrelated. Change in one area changes another. When technology changes the method of working and amount of wealth generated other areas in life are transformed. People begin to question the existing order, see new ways of doing things and relate differently to one another. Everyday living such as sexuality, music and food reflect these changes.

The most dramatic change that we are familiar with is the Industrial Revolution. The Industrial Revolution changed the way goods were produced, distributed, sold and consumed. Modern advertising, mass transportation systems and global warfare developed as a result of changes that the Industrial Revolution brought. It wasn't just the presence of physical goods that changed. Rather, it was the entire spectrum of human behavior that changed.

The late 20th century and early 21st century is experiencing a similar type of transformation based on the introduction of the microchip. The microchip has ushered in a new wave of inventions from the cellular phone, camcorder, hand-held computer, Internet and a wide array of other communication devices. Although originating in the United States, developments in electronics is increasingly being done and performed in Asia and other parts of the world. If one were to turn over any electronic device one would likely find Made in China, Korea or Malaysia. Like the Industrial Revolution, the Information Revolution is spreading and transforming cultures in ways previously not imagined.

Before exploring the current transformation of the world political economy it is useful to examine the rise of the Western world upon which the current world economy is based upon. Future developments are born out of the previous existing order. It is useful to examine the characteristics that led to previous changes in the ranking of nations in order to understand what will arise in the future.

The rise of the Western world has been the defining feature of the last several hundred years. Since the formation of the capitalist market in the 13th century Western powers have dominated the world political economy. A succession of Western powers dominated world affairs as one Western nation advanced and declined followed by another that took its place.

Looking forward from 1500 one might have predicted that China or other region outside of Europe would have led the world. Yet, European powers would come to dominate the world political economy. A variety of circumstances converged that allowed Europe to dominate. The Protestant work ethic is one general theory that attempted to explain why the West arose. Others have proposed similar theories that attempt to combine the religious, cultural, political and economic circumstances that allowed the dominance of the West. World systems theories (e.g. Immanuel Wallerstein) view dependency on a core region as central while developmental theories embrace free trade and markets.

Europe possessed a number of factors that allowed it to surpass more developed regions at the time. Both Africa and Asia had more developed cultures in several areas. However, while China was inward looking and bureaucratic Europe looked outward and saw fierce rivalry between European countries. Abundant water ports and centrality to Africa, Middle East and Asia also allowed Europe to explore, trade and develop technologies that would propel it to dominance. These factors were among many that contributed to Europe's rise to power.

During the 1700s the rational and scientific beliefs of the Enlightenment, growing out of the Industrial Revolution, advanced European power. One technological invention fueled another. Even more important, economic progress changed every other area of society: social, political, cultural and religious. The Reformation and other movements were related to the economic changes Europe underwent. Changing economic circumstances led to changes in people's outlooks in many areas of life. Eventually, vast areas of society were transformed.

By the late 1800s European powers extended their influence to every region of the globe. It was said that the sun never set on the British Empire. Other European countries had influence in Asia, Africa and Middle East. No area of the globe was outside Europe's influence. European customs, technology and culture spread to other regions bringing transformation. Africa's current borders are the creation of European powers saying how they wanted Africa organized.

During the time of European dominance, the most influential power came from northern Europe. Specifically, Anglo-Saxon nations led. Great Britain inherited power from the Netherlands. Other European nations played catch up with Great Britain during the Industrial Revolution. Great Britain developed a high concentration of manufacturing in many high value goods. During the early 19th century it was the United States that exported raw materials and imported finished goods from Great Britain.

World War I eroded Europe's belief of central importance (much like Vietnam did for the United States). Specifically, World War I eroded Great Britain's status as leading power. It was not obvious at first that Great Britain was in decline as no national currency immediately replaced the pound sterling between World War I and II. However, manufacturing and economic power were shifting to a rising power on the other side of the Atlantic.

The United States continued Europe's Enlightenment and Industrial Revolution. To a large degree, the United States developed out of Western beliefs. The French Revolution, Adam Smith and Christian beliefs permeated throughout American culture. Those from southern and eastern Europe (e.g. Italy and Poland) would take prominence later in American history. Great Britain was most influential in determining the direction of the New World.

America had several dominant strains of thought that were present at the nation's inception. Alexander Hamilton believed in a strong central government and supported a national bank and the development of industry. Thomas Jefferson desired a decentralized agrarian society based on farmers. The Civil War highlighted these differences. These two major differences in outlook continue to this day. Republicans generally support state's right and small government. Democrats are inheritors of Hamilton's desire for stronger government (ironically, the political beliefs of each party reversed over time).

Over time, particularly after the Civil War, the United States developed a strong industrial base validating Hamilton's desire for an industrial society. The Northeast and Midwest developed the greatest concentration of manufacturing. Automobiles, aircraft, subways, steel framed skyscrapers and nylon were invented. As a result, other changes in American society resulted: mass education, labor movements and social welfare programs. Perhaps the most important was the change in social organization leading to hierarchical organizations with well-defined structure. This profoundly changed how business, labor and government were organized.

Even though late 19th century American industrialists amassed power based on a public philosophy of individualistic competition the United States government contributed to economic growth through measures such as the Homestead Act and railroad financing. In addition, some corporations took a paternalistic approach toward workers. In other words, the myth of rugged individualism was just that. Americans tend to emphasize individual influences and de-emphasize the social ones. This thinking tends to distort the understanding of American history.

Nevertheless, compared with Europe and Asia, the approach taken by the United States remained laissez-faire. Marxism and socialism never took hold in the United States as it did in Europe. While many European nations developed social democracy the United States maintained its belief in capitalism. In the minds of many Americans laissez-faire attitudes prevailed where business was left unfettered by government.

However, the severity of the Great Depression altered the attitudes of Americans toward government. Periodic booms and busts had occurred during American history. Yet, the Great Depression saw capitalism unable to rejuvenate itself. John Maynard Keynes, a British economist, provided an economic framework to understand the Great Depression. Keynes understood the Great Depression as resulting from a lack of demand. In other words, supply and demand did not automatically equalize under capitalism as classical economists predicted. Unemployment soared while prices collapsed.

As a result, Americans turned to Franklin Roosevelt during the 1932 presidential elections. Roosevelt promoted government as a means to buttress and maintain capitalism. The National Recovery Act, Social Security and minimum wage were started during this time. Many more Americans began to see government as a beneficial and necessary sector to support capitalism. It is said that Roosevelt saved capitalism from itself.

In the meantime, New York State, where Franklin Roosevelt had previously been governor, grew in prominence. New York City and its surrounding areas took advantage of the electric motor to become the dominant region in the United States during the 20th century. Other regions of the United States developed but it was this region that developed the greatest concentration of wealth and propelled the United States after World War II. Those on Madison Avenue created national advertising that would be filtered through the eyes of those living in this region.

World War II propelled the United States to world leadership and helped create the framework for the next several decades. It wasn't just victory but the synergistic effort of all sectors of the United States that contributed toward victory. War production involved all sectors of the American economy: business, government and labor. To a degree greater than ever before Americans took a cooperative outlook toward their society.

The Cold War maintained the need for increased levels of involvement between business, government and labor. The Central Intelligence

Agency, Defense Department and other Cold War agencies demanded cooperation from a wide array of institutions. In the meantime, policy makers desired high levels of consumption to maintain high levels of employment for social stability. The Cold War continued the need for greater cooperation between Americans.

After World War II the United States maintained hegemony much like Great Britain did a century earlier. This period can be referred to as a period of Pax Americana where the United States provided a stable world political framework. Bretton Woods (1944) started the process of forming world institutions under American leadership. The General Agreement on Tariffs and Trade (GATT) and other world institutions under American leadership provided the guiding hand for leadership after World War II.

This golden era continued into the early 1970s. However, Japan and Western Europe were recovering from World War II destruction and were beginning to complement America's role in the world. Beginning in the late 1960s imports would make inroads into the American market. Americans experienced defeat in Vietnam. Oil sheiks would challenge American hegemony by dramatically increasing the price of crude oil. President Richard Nixon removed the gold standard and implemented price controls to stabilize the world economy. Numerous setbacks in the 1970s eroded America's influence throughout the world.

The election of Ronald Reagan in 1980 temporarily inflated the influence of the United States. Reagan promised Morning in America and a country Standing Tall. Yet, Reaganomics did not fundamentally alter the shifting power away from the United States and toward Asia and Europe. Japan moved upscale to challenge Cadillac and Lincoln while Mercedes and other European brands ate away at American market share.

In December 1991 the collapse of the Soviet Union and its satellites brought confirmation of capitalism's superiority. Yet, the success of Japan and Western Europe raised questions as to the superiority of the

American system. Other countries had lower crime rates, larger middle classes and higher quality products. Some Americans said that the Cold War was over and Japan and Germany had won.

At the beginning of the 21st century the world economy is undergoing a transformation on a scale not seen before. The microchip is the most recent invention that is propelling the next technological revolution based on information. Information processing of all types is being manipulated, transformed and changed due to this technology. Cell phones, Internet transactions, 500-channel television and personal computers all have in common the ability to handle greater amounts of information in greatly expanded ways. Graphic design, geographic information systems (GIS) and computer-aided drafting are only some of the fields being created by the microchip.

Many assume that power will remain with the United States and the West. Yet, this belief is untested. The microchip, personal computer and Internet originated in the United States. However, a nation that develops particular technology is not necessarily the one to exploit it. Japan has been a master at taking technology from others and improving upon it to develop still more technologies. Other Asian nations have followed in Japan's footsteps by successfully manufacturing quality goods.

Many Americans corporations have shifted production overseas while they perform services such as finance, marketing and retail. However, many services rely on manufacturing. Previously, Great Britain relied on services to compensate for the loss of manufacturing and found this approach failed to balance trade. Those nations that maintained the primacy of manufacturing such as Germany have kept a favorable balance of trade.

Recently, China has dramatically increased its export of manufactured goods. Many quality and increasingly sophisticated goods are being produced by China. The United States is experiencing larger trade deficits with China similar to those found with Japan. China has not yet entered high-value goods such as supercomputers and aircraft but is demanding the transfer of technology in exchange for access to its markets (as Japan had earlier). It is important to remember that Japan's rise from wartime destruction only took several decades. The same might happen with China on a much larger scale.

Furthermore, all of Asia from India to the Philippines is rapidly growing. India is promoting software and the availability of English-speaking professionals to other countries. Indonesia, Malaysia and other Asian nations are experiencing rapid growth. It is likely that Asia's economic success is generating synergy and will advance this region further.

An interesting phenomenon is the globalization of manufacturing throughout the world. Sophisticated production is rapidly being shifted and moved throughout the world. It is not uncommon to see components made in Japan, assembled in China and packaged in the United States. American firms started moving production abroad in the 1970s to reduce labor costs. Recently, other nations have followed suit. However, an important difference is the manner in which this is done. Other countries have not sacrificed so many manufacturing jobs and transferred crucial technology.

Many influential commentators in the United States believe that a 'borderless' world is being created where nationality does not matter. Many American corporations accept this role by moving production across the globe without great concern for the home base. It is assumed that the United States can maintain leadership without having concern for the home base.

However, history and current events do not support this belief in a borderless world. Nationality does matter. Before World War I the world experienced a rapid increase in trade between nations. Great Britain assumed that its leading power status would remain. Instead, growth rates did not converge between Great Britain and the industrializing nations of Germany and the United States. Rather, Germany and the United States (among others) surpassed Great Britain's standard of living. Neither did borders disappear as some thought possible at the turn of the 20th century when world trade accelerated. Instead, World War I erupted in 1914.

In many respects, the world at the beginning of the 21st century is similar to the beginning of the 20th. World trade has significantly increased. New technologies have spawned changes in thinking about a new millennium. A leading power is experiencing dramatic changes in its culture and experiencing an influx of foreign ideas. Previously unheard names are now familiar such as Toyota, Honda and Sony.

It is understandable to assume that past rankings in the world will continue and that the leaders now will be similar to the leaders in the future. However, history shows that change can be discontinuous. Dramatic shifts in power can and do occur. History provides clues as to what will transpire over the first half of the 21st century. Events do not happen in a vacuum. By carefully understanding history and basic social change an outline of the future can be understood.

It is likely that the three major economic blocs of power (Asia, Europe and the United States) will continue to remain influential. Communism and its socialist variants will not likely be revived. The influence of the microchip on society will continue. Globalization will remain important in manufacturing, culture and politics. And in some respects the United States will disproportionately influence world events.

Select nations in Eastern Europe, Latin America and other regions will approach standards of living found among the wealthiest. Goods will increasingly be made in India, Brazil or Hungary. However, many areas of the globe will remain poor relative to Asia, Europe and North America.

However, the most dramatic event will be the entry into the Western club of affluence many nations from Asia. Asia made a remarkable rise from 1950 through 2000 quadrupling its standard of living. Asia will likely grow to a point where it will contend for world leadership. Will this rate of progress in Asia continue? Could it replace the West as the leading power?

Chapter I discusses the American Century. What circumstances allowed the United States to arise to world prominence after World War II? The difficulties during the 1960s and 1970s are discussed as well as the American response of laissez-faire economics. The prospects for the United States during the 21st century are outlined as well as needed remedies.

Chapter II discusses the two overriding concerns of wealth and its importance for leadership in the 21st century: efficiency and equality. The two economic statistics used to measure efficiency and equality is discussed: productivity and the Gini Index. These are related to the Group of Seven (G7) providing glimpses of future developments.

Chapter III discusses the general concept of how wealth is generated. Both competition and cooperation are viewed as central in generating the greatest economic wealth for all. The idea of economic democracy is put forth as a form of organizing society that is both fair and prosperous for future generations.

Chapter IV discusses the world in the 21st century and who will pull ahead and who will fall behind. A detailed discussion of the United States and its social stratification will be explored and the implications for its society well into the 21st century.

About the Author details the work history and education of the author and how it influenced the writing of *Wealth in the 21st Century*. Every book is influenced by the life history of its author.

The overreaching goal of this book is to provide readers with some basic information important to life in the 21st century. Many of the day-to-day decisions that we make are strongly influenced by the larger, but harder to grasp world of social change created by technology. Career decisions, child rearing, community health and politics among many others are strongly influenced by these large and increasingly global events. *Wealth in the 21st Century* hopes to decipher some of these workings.

I

The American Century

Henry Luce, editor of *Time* magazine, coined the phrase American Century during 1941. Previously, the United States declined the role of world leader by failing to join the League of Nations after World War I. The period between World War I and II resulted in no real world leader and the rise of fascism and communism in Europe. However, the Great Depression and World War II would change the United States.

During the Great Depression the United States was called the sleeping giant. The United States had rapidly industrialized after the Civil War developing many inventions such as nylon, the radio, the Model T assembly line and mechanized agriculture. Cities like Chicago, Detroit and Los Angeles grew many times beyond their original size. Standard Oil, Ford and General Electric became dominant corporations wielding much power.

Capitalism experienced periodic downturns when business would experience a sharp contraction. However, business would rebound and return to previous economic levels of output. The Great Depression proved to be different. Capitalism did not right itself from the stock market crash, creating a run on banks and business failures. Classical economists assumed that supply and demand would eventually eliminate any economic slump as prices reached equilibrium. Government intervention was not an option. Income taxes were only introduced in

1913 and then only on the very wealthy. The individualistic nature of the United States supported unfettered competition. However, the length and duration of the Great Depression challenged these beliefs.

1. Keynesian Economics: 1932–1968

Increases in productivity during the late 19th and early 20th century eventually resulted in a surplus of goods and a lack of buyers. For example, throughout the 1920s the price of a Model T steadily declined. However, many worker wages did not keep pace with the increase in production. Techniques such as advertising attempted to increase the demand for the growing array of products created by manufacturers. However, this did not resolve the fundamental oversupply and lack of demand.

Eventually, this imbalance in the economy led to the Great Depression. Business was not able to provide expansion of the economy. Starting with the stock market crash in 1929 unemployment increased to nearly one quarter of the American workforce. Worldwide, unemployment dramatically increased while trade between nations decreased. Capitalism had periodic downturns but never for such an extended period of time on such a global scale.

John Maynard Keynes, a British economist, understood the Great Depression as resulting from a lack of demand. In other worlds, markets did not automatically reach equilibrium as classical economists had predicted. Keynes wrote that government investment would be necessary for full employment. Some assumed that increasing tariffs erected by nations created the Great Depression. However, tariffs were not the cause of the Great Depression. Collapsing prices due to excess supply created a vicious cycle. Eventually, mass unemployment resulted.

Herbert Hoover, elected in 1928, was unable to convince Americans of the viability of Republican policy. Americans elected Franklin Roosevelt in 1932 and changed the political landscape in a manner periodically done in American history. Roosevelt challenged laissez-faire economics and proposed the New Deal. Franklin Roosevelt introduced an alphabet soup of government programs such as the CCC (Civilian Conservation Corps) and NRA (National Recovery Act).

More than anything, the entry of the United States into World War II with the bombing of Pearl Harbor in 1941 finally created full employment and an expanding economy. Wartime production demanded collective investment from business, labor and government. All sectors of the American economy were harnessed in a way that laissez-faire economics failed to appreciate. Unemployment, ten percent in 1940, reached near zero during World War II while scarcity of products forced high levels of savings.

World War II victory confirmed and reinforced America's belief of exceptionality. Returning GI's from the European and Pacific theatres saw the superiority of American efforts. The fear that large numbers of returning soldiers combined with a fall in wartime production would result in mass unemployment and a return of the Great Depression never materialized. Instead, the United States would embark on a period of economic prosperity.

Part of this post-World War II success can be attributed to the efforts of intelligent American leaders who saw the necessity to implement a workable framework for the world political economy. In the short-term the Marshall and Truman Plans helped Europe repel communism and stabilize its economies. The Bretton Woods agreement helped provide the workings for the post-World War II world political economy. The General Agreement on Tariffs and Trade (GATT) among other world institutions encouraged American-style leadership for a generation. Not surprisingly, the headquarters for the United Nations was located in New York City.

Both Europe and Japan had to recover from wartime destruction. The United States had the world markets to itself. The United States could build on its existing industrial base that was left unscathed by

World War II. The largest American firms (Fortune 500) were able to compete mostly with domestic competitors. Foreign competition was largely absent and ignored. The few products the United States did import were specialty foreign goods such as the Volkswagen Beetle.

The Cold War maintained the need for greater cooperation that grew during World War II. Defense and space programs, intelligence agencies and interstate highways were financed and proposed by a mixture of private and public sectors. The traditional conflict between labor and management was muted by an unwritten social contract that more or less guaranteed rising wages and employment.

Underlying these policies was the importance that Keynesian economics took place in the minds of American policy makers. Influential Americans implemented Keynesian economics in the form of a 'mixed' economy that provided full employment and rising wages through consumption. All sectors of the economy (government, labor and business) were viewed as important to the economy. Laissez-faire economics was pushed to the side in favor of this form of social cooperation.

Throughout both Democratic and Republican administrations the New Deal was maintained and expanded. Americans came to accept that business, labor and government had legitimate roles to play in the economy. Furthermore, economics, politics and society were seen as intertwined in promoting the general welfare of the nation. For example, President John Kennedy forced the steel industry to hold prices in order to keep the unwritten social contract between business, labor and government.

Eventually, a new governing elite came into existence: the liberal establishment. The liberal establishment was comprised of New Deal Democrats and Rockefeller Republicans who comprised the 'vital center.' One could draw an oval from Boston to Chicago with New York City as its center that defined the core support for the liberal establishment. The industrial Northeast with manufacturing as its basis dominated national affairs and maintained Pax Americana.

As happens with ascending regions, cultural, political and economic power flowed from the Northeast. Advertising and marketing came mainly from Madison Avenue in New York City. Popular media often portrayed life as seen from this region. Levittown epitomized the growing suburban middle class. Unfortunately, one effect of the 'effortless economic prosperity' was increasingly myopic vision.

Lyndon Johnson's presidential victory over Republican contender Barry Goldwater in 1964 was overwhelming. Johnson proposed the Great Society program as well as Civil Rights legislation. Many new social programs were created during this time. An expanding economy provided jobs in a wide array of areas from the space program, social welfare and Fortune 500 companies. The Vietnam conflict had not yet arisen. Americans increasingly saw institutions (particularly, government) as the key to the 'effortless economic prosperity.' Some thought that anything was possible.

The liberal establishment had two dangerous illusions that would undermine its authority during and after the 1960s. One was a belief that inequalities in American society could be abolished without hard choices (e.g. taxes). The other was that the United States could use its military power to make the world conform to its world outlook (e.g. Vietnam). Social welfare policy such as job training failed to understand the structural problems of poverty. The nationalist conflict in Vietnam was understood only in terms of the Cold War.

During the late 1960s a significant cultural change was occurring based on the coming of age of a new generation: baby boomers. Returning GIs from World War II had large families afterwards resulting in a bulge of births. From 1946 through 1964 a new generation was being born that would change the face of the cultural landscape. Other nations would experience youthful protest but the greatest increase in births for this generation occurred in the United States.

The desire for nonconformity and protest took place among small and disenchanted groups of youth. The roots of protest occurred in the

1950s but never took hold in this conformist period of American history. Prosperity likely contributed to the growing self-confidence of youth during the mid-1960s. Interestingly, protests started at elite colleges and universities among the most affluent. Many baby boomers from blue-collar or state universities did not actively protest. Many who now write about the 1960s come from the same affluent backgrounds as the activists and gloss over the nonparticipation by many of the baby boomer generation.

The Civil Rights Movement galvanized the efforts of many protesters and created the training needed for other areas of protest. Some who started in the Civil Rights Movement later joined the youth, women's and Native American movements in the increasingly fragmented political landscape. The overarching goals of economic democracy, reducing poverty and concern for the general welfare of the nation became subordinated to the goals of increasingly issue-specific groups.

As the 1960s continued the Vietnam conflict took more and more center stage in the activities of student protesters. Vietnam protesters who might have shown support for government policy such as a guaranteed minimum income and democratization of the workplace began to turn against government. In the meantime, conservatives such as Ronald Reagan (elected governor of California in 1966 and 1970) were attacking from the right. The 'vital center' was beginning to implode as the result of unattainable goals and hypocrisy.

At first glance, it appeared that the New Left and Students for a Democratic Society (SDS) were gaining ground. The popular imagination portrays the 1960s as being dominated by leftist events: the Summer of Love, Woodstock and Earth Day. However, the Sixties upheaval was led by a minority of upper-middle class students and intellectuals centered on the East and West Coasts. Most Americans did not share the aspirations of this affluent group. The Movement failed to understand the character and tradition of the United Sates.

Research shows that the majority of baby boomers did not join or share in the aspirations of the student leaders. Just as during the 1980s the influence of the religious right was exaggerated, the influence of the small group of student protesters on the left was overemphasized. A minority of baby boom protesters maintained their beliefs. For most baby boomers protest never materialized in the first place.

Historically, American society is very cyclical and does not move in a linear fashion. Most Americans were unaware that history was moving toward the end rather than the beginning of the liberal movement that began with Franklin Roosevelt. Student leaders may have been the least aware. Student protest leaders failed to understand the workings of everyday American life. Furthermore, growing up during prosperous times further narrowed their understanding of the United States.

The Sixties Movement fragmented into issue-specific concerns: the environment, Native American concerns, women's issues and marijuana legalization among others. Eventually, the youth movement that developed to remove liberal hypocrisy and fight for social justice evolved into an individualistic spiritual quest revolving around fashions and attitudes. Self-actualization and self-fulfillment became the central focus for the Me Generation. Mainstream America would soon join the youth in their version of self-expression during the 1970s. Some student protesters during the 1980s became supporters of the Reagan Revolution in an attempt to reinvigorate their idealism.

Nonetheless, some protesters understood American society at a deeper level that has since been lost. Some understood how Americans do not start out at the same starting line and that these inequalities strongly influence success. Simply providing increased opportunities does not level the playing field. Some saw the need for democratization of the workplace where political equality would be extended to the economic realm. However, Vietnam engulfed much of these efforts.

The real upheaval, predicted by Kevin Phillips in *The Emerging Republican Majority*, was the silent majority's populist revolt that supported Richard Nixon. Phillips, reviewing United States political history, convincingly argued that political upheavals occurred every 32 or 36 years (approximately the span of one generation). He predicted that 1968 would be such a watershed year. However, the shift would be to the right, not left.

From 1968 through 2000, every president has come from the growing conservative regions of the West and South. Furthermore, only two Democratic Presidents were elected (Carter and Clinton-themselves conservative Democrats from the South). George W. Bush, Republican governor from Texas, will likely win the 2000 presidential elections. Since the 1960s, Americans have turned back to a more individualistic society based on small government, low-density suburbs and a small business service economy. Not until the 2004 elections will Americans choose to return to a more cooperative form of society.

Following the tumultuous 1960s the United States experienced significant setbacks in the 1970s: Vietnam, Watergate and the 1973–74 Oil Embargo. More than anything, Vietnam accelerated the loss of faith in institutions (particularly government) dividing the nation and ending consensus about America's role in the world. However, overlooked by many Americans, was the changing balance of power in the world economy when foreign imports began to erode America's mass manufacturing dominance.

2. The 1973 Economic Slowdown

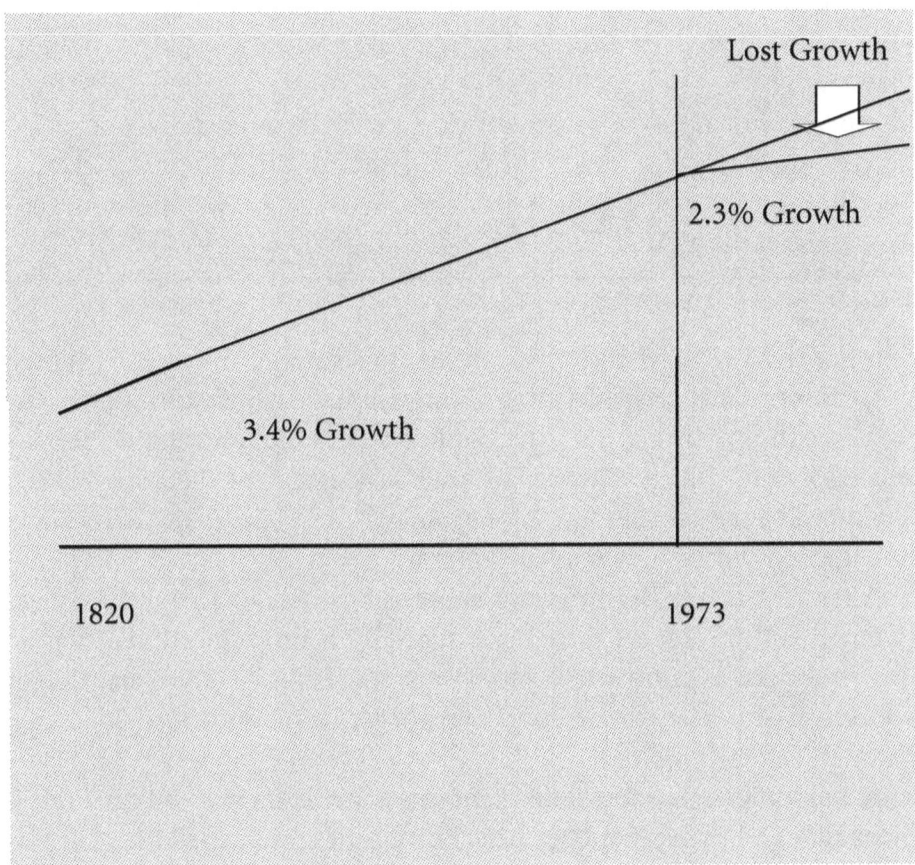

The End of Affluence, Madrick

'This graph, then, is the economic expression of why we feel the way we do today. In the shaded area (arrow) lie our lost jobs, falling and stagnating wages, eroding markets, closed factories, rising levels of poverty, insecure pensions, and reduced home ownership. Though we blame it on other things, the widening gap between what had been our normal rate of growth for a century and the actual performance of the economy is the main source of the American public's declining confidence, which has shown up in survey after survey since the early 1970s.' *The End of Affluence*, Madrick

Since the 1820s, when American manufacturers competed with high value imports from Great Britain, America increasingly dominated the world economy through its success in mass manufacturing. America's success came from economies of scale as a result of its large market. Taylor's Theory of Scientific Management and Henry Ford's assembly line formed the basis of mass production.

After World War II, prosperity enabled business to accept the collective bargaining process bringing a truce with unions and creating an unwritten social contract of increasing wages and employment. This collective agreement between government, labor and business lasted through the early 1970s.

Other nations developed different manufacturing methods as a result of smaller and fragmented markets. Europeans emphasized the craft tradition and developing niche products. Japan emphasized cooperation and quality in manufacturing due to its limited geographical size and dependence on imported raw materials. After World War II both Europe and Japan built a modern and tightly managed manufacturing base with lean production and lower costs based on flexible manufacturing.

Starting in the 1960s, increasing standards of living and education created demand for higher quality goods in greater variety while energy costs placed a premium on production costs. These conditions favored flexible manufacturing techniques in Japan and Europe. At the same time, wages in the United States were far higher. The United States, having made substantial financial and psychological investment in mass production, found it difficult to make the change from mass to flexible manufacturing. American manufacturers began to lose market share. Profitability declined from 9.4% in 1966 to 6.4% in 1973.

Not until the 1973–74 recession did the effects of increased foreign competition become widely felt by Americans. The 1973–74 recession marked a distinct break with America's previous fast economic growth rate. For the first time in American history (including the Great Depression) wages stagnated or declined for many. However, unlike the Great Depression, the economic growth rate did not slow enough to create real social, political or economic upheaval.

At first, OPEC oil price increases and stagflation (high unemployment and high inflation) were blamed. Some experts believed that America's slow growth after 1973 was simply due to America's unusual dominance of the world economy after World War II. However, the growth rate before World War II dating back to the 1820's was similar. It was the economic growth rate after 1973 that was unusually low.

Many Americans perceived that somewhere along the road at this time the United States took a wrong turn. These feelings ebb and flow with recoveries and recessions. During the economic recoveries in the 1980s and 1990s Americans were more optimistic about their nation. However, recessions that started in the early 1980s and 1990s punctured the 'don't worry, be happy' attitude characteristic of many Americans. Loss of faith in institutions, a rise in poverty and a general feeling of dissatisfaction correspond with this slowdown in economic growth. In other words, economic growth paved the way for faith in the American Dream rather than the reverse. However, most Americans (60 percent of white Americans in a fall 1994 survey) blamed our problems on deteriorating moral values.

The reaction of many Americans was to turn inwards. When the ability to influence the physical world became blocked, many people turned to spirituality, psychotherapy, new religions and family values for meaning. The Power of Positive Thinking held many Americans. However, this positive thinking prevented understanding of America's predicament and placed blame on each other. Most importantly, government had been targeted as the cause of America's problems and reducing government as the solution.

Given the volatility of American opinion, diagnosis of its ills becomes difficult if even the existence of these ills is in question. Vietnam, Watergate and the 1960s protests overshadowed America's loss of manufacturing dominance. However, it was the introduction of flexible manufacturing and its threat to mass manufacturing that led to America's declining fortunes. For manufacturing provided the foundation for many other aspects of American society: jobs, family income and community cohesion.

3. Laissez-Faire Economics: 1968–2004

'(Vietnam destroyed) the once near-universal faith in the uniqueness of our values and their relevance around the world.' Henry Kissinger

In general, American corporations had two choices to deal with declining profitability as a result of flexible manufacturing: cost cutting or increased investment. Investment in higher value manufacturing would have emphasized worker training, creating a more cooperative work arrangement between management and labor and a long-term focus. On the other hand, cost cutting involved reducing wages and dissolving unions in favor of 'flexible labor.' Both can work. However, only the former leads to a higher standard of living.

American corporations decided to cut costs. Corporations began a frenzy of buying and selling creating conglomerates in hopes of maintaining cash flow and high profitability. Product lines were diluted, poor management decisions were implemented and corporate management became overstaffed. Large workforce layoffs and relocation of operations to right-to-work states followed. Until the early 1980s, American firms could claim high wages were to blame for declining fortunes. However, by the mid-1980s Germany and Japan had higher manufacturing wages. While Japan moved upstream to produce complex electronic equipment American firms moved production to Mexico. While Germany emphasized high-quality luxury automobiles Detroit reduced its workforce.

Given the history and structure of the United State's economy, corporations may not have had much leeway in the course of action they took. The United State's financial system emphasized short-term profitability. American labor and management have traditionally been adversarial. A nation's cumulative history biases it toward certain decisions and not others. Real change can be very difficult without crisis.

Ronald Reagan was elected in 1980 largely due to the declining fortunes of the United State's economy. Reagan changed public policy similar to laissez-faire economics: tax reductions, deregulation and reduced government investment. Not coincidentally, Reagan hung a portrait of Calvin Coolidge in the White House signifying this change in philosophy.

Ronald Reagan held the imagination of Americans more than any president since John Kennedy or Franklin Roosevelt. Reagan won in presidential landslides in both 1980 and 1984. If any leader represented American beliefs it was Ronald Reagan. Reagan was a master communicator that weaved fact with fiction in creating a memorable impression of American history. Morning in America and Standing Tall were the central beliefs of Reagan.

Unfortunately, Reaganomics did not revitalize American industry. Rather, it accelerated the demise of manufacturing by encouraging cost cutting. Furthermore, Reagan practiced a form of Keynesian economics through large government deficits. Reagan accelerated negative attitudes toward government by burdening government with large deficits. Reagan's response was that government wasn't the solution, but the problem.

The end result was the discrediting of government and reliance on business for investment and growth. Investment did not substantially increase. Neither did government spending appreciably decrease. Furthermore, Reaganomics was hard to sustain without the Gipper as president.

Other than Margaret Thatcher's policies in Great Britain, few nations followed America's laissez-faire approach. Asian and European nations viewed business, government and labor as interrelated and part of the same social capital. Business helped train labor. Labor actively contributed to business productivity. Government provided investment for both. The American government's response to the loss of manufacturing was that free markets and free trade would determine winners and losers; not much could or should be done. The United States did not develop an industrial policy as European or Asian governments did.

Instead, American leaders emphasized individual responsibility. Specifically, Americans were told to obtain further education. However, this puts the cart before the horse. It was expanding opportunities in the job market that created demand for more education, not the other way around. Some students have found that with lower returns on educational achievement (entry-level college graduate wages dropped 7% from 1989–97), dropping out made more economic sense. There is no indication that Americans lack education. No large area of jobs needs to be filled.

Not surprisingly, after 1975, the American economy's ability to generate good paying jobs diminished significantly:

1. **Manufacturing jobs** (particularly those that paid a middle-class income) disappeared. Previously, improvements in manufacturing productivity did not come at the expense of fewer manufacturing jobs. Employment in high-paid sectors of manufacturing for blue-collar males decreased from 57% to 36% between 1968 and 1986.

2. **Service jobs** increased. Although some offered higher pay, most were lower. Employment in retail/services for blue-collar males increased from 30% to 48% between 1968 and 1986.

3. **High-technology jobs** have been created, but not at a rate fast enough to offset jobs lost in manufacturing. Out of the top twenty occupations generating job growth, only one could be considered high-tech (systems analyst).

In summary, there has been a large increase in the demand for low-paid service jobs while high-paid manufacturing jobs disappeared. As pay for male high-school graduates decreased (28% from the mid 1970s through late 1980s) this had a significant impact on the ability of these graduates to successfully start families.

The overall trend is confusing because of two conflicting trends: a shift toward higher-paying *occupations* (managers and professionals) but a shift toward lower-paying *industries* (service and retail). Political and economic leaders frequently mention the positive occupational shift, but ignore the more important negative industrial shift.

The end of the Cold War did not rejuvenate faith in laissez-faire economics. One phrase heard after the collapse of the Soviet Union and its empire was that the Cold War was over and Japan and Germany had won. George Bush inherited the 1990-91 recession where white-collar job losses outnumbered blue-collar for the first time. Bush lost to Bill Clinton even after overwhelmingly winning the Gulf War. Labor candidate Tony Blair would win in Great Britain while Canadians voted all but a handful of Progressive Conservatives out of office.

Nonetheless, the election of these new leaders did not appreciably change public policy. For example, Bill Clinton's national health coverage was defeated in 1993. Clinton called for 'the end of big government as we know it.' George W. Bush, the likely successor to Clinton in 2000, promotes a compassionate conservatism that does not challenge laissez-faire policy.

By the 1990s, the wages of American workers were no longer the highest. Only by measuring wages in terms of purchasing power did wages equal other developed nations. Only two other nations experienced near zero growth rates (Canada and Denmark). The United States was the only industrial nation where wages declined in absolute amounts. Furthermore, the United States had the smallest middle-class of any industrial nation (for example, read the article 'What boom? Two-thirds of USA stuck in 1973,' *USA Today*, November 12, 1998).

The upturn in productivity during the late 1990s had many prominent publications (e.g. *Business Week* and *Wall Street Journal*) proclaiming a New Economy based on productivity gains from information technology. An array of new products and technologies based on information processing seems to finally have produced positive results for improving the output per worker. Indeed, productivity had increased after 1996.

However, the United States is using information technology in the end stages of production (e.g. retail and distribution) rather than production itself. In other words, gains are coming in the peripheral areas of production rather than building new productive capability. These gains coincided with market share loss in a wide array of industries: aircraft, cellular phones and computer manufacturing. Furthermore, the United States was running huge trade deficits, an indicator that it was not selling goods the world wanted to buy.

The Internet and related information technologies will likely prove to be a less important player in the 21st century than many believe. The Internet and communication technologies present several problems: a skewed set of jobs providing fewer middle paying jobs, less job creation compared to manufacturing and failure to reverse America's negative trade balance. Information technology shares many of the weaknesses that services exhibit.

It is unlikely that Asia's good fortunes over the last 25 years have suddenly declined while America's has improved in a matter of only a few years. Japan and China continue to amass large trade surpluses while the United States accumulates large trade deficits. It is possible that Asia is experiencing a crisis in lack of demand similar to what the United States experienced in the 1930s. However, Asia (like the United States after the Great Depression) will likely come out stronger than before.

Anglo-Saxon finance and its demand for maximization on the return on capital is the driving force behind laissez-faire capitalism. Global finance (e.g. International Monetary Fund and World Bank) is promoting the Anglo-Saxon model. As long as the United States can be the buyer of last resort the system will remain afloat. Needless to say, the day when America will no longer be able to perform this role will arrive. A new system of international institutions will be needed.

The most successful nations are following Japan's model that place controls on capital (for example, Mexico unsuccessfully used the laissez-faire model). China does not allow its currency to be convertible. The Asian crisis during 1997 cautioned many about the problems of Anglo-Saxon institutions. Many see America's set of institutions as being predatory and counterproductive to the well being of the world's political economy.

Finally, America's slow economic growth is similar to other Anglo-Saxon nations: Great Britain, Canada, Australia and New Zealand. All of these nations have experienced the slowest growth rates among the developed nations. America, sharing culture and institutions with these nations, is likely sharing the structural problems leading to slow growth. It is quite possible that the Anglo-Saxon economic model will not be the leader in the 21st century.

4. American Economics in the 21st Century

'The United States of the 1990s…is following a pattern broadly similar to that in the other leading world powers we have been discussing. Some of the symptoms are economic, some cultural, some mixed. By using the examples of Rome, Spain, the Netherlands, Britain, and the United States, and listing the characteristics widespread enough to occur in three or four out of the five nations during their decline stages, one comes up with the following:

Economic	Mixed Cultural and Economic	Cultural
*Economic polarization	*Declining middle class	*Increased sophistication in culture and arts
*Concentration of wealth	*Deteriorating cities	*Luxury and permissiveness
*Rising debt	*Declining quality of education	*Complaints about foreign influence and loss of old patriotism
*Higher taxes		
*Relative decline in manufacturing	*Increasing internationalism of elites	
*Increasing speculation and the rise of finance	*Increasingly burdensome national capital	*Complaints about moral decay

Arrogant Capital, Phillips

The United States has entered a period of relative decline similar to previous leading powers and will likely continue to do so unless a wholesale reorganization of its society is attempted. Many will continue to deny or evade questions of decline and allow the current drift to continue. Yet the parallels with previous leading powers like Great Britain is uncanny.

The United States is most similar to Great Britain in terms of its institutions. Therefore, a comparison with this former leading power is most appropriate. At the turn of the 20th century Great Britain began to lose manufacturing to the United States and Germany. Similar to the United States today, many British thought that services would replace manufacturing. Eventually, Great Britain reached a point where the export of services did not compensate for the import of manufactured goods. The United States has already reached this point.

Furthermore, many British relied on finance to compensate for declining profitability of industry. London became a center of world finance for a considerable length of time. In a similar vein, Wall Street has attracted investors from around the globe as stocks dramatically increase in valuation at the end of the 20th century. However, one should not confuse profitability with productivity. In Great Britain finance hindered reinvestment into industry for fear of lower returns much as it has in the United States.

Business, government and personal debt increased in both nations. Great Britain could no longer use the pound sterling to buttress the world economy after World War I. After the Cold War the United States relied on subsidization from its allies to fight the Gulf War. Both nations experienced deteriorating trade balances. The United States is alone in experiencing such large trade deficits.

Likewise, both Great Britain and the United States simultaneously experienced an increase in poverty and wealth while the middle class became proportionately smaller. Class divisions widened while opportunities for good paying jobs diminished for all but those at the top. Deterioration of cities, general decay and worsening public services resulted.

Finally, there were cries about moral decay in both Great Britain and the United States. Complaints about a lack of patriotism, teenage pregnancy, venereal disease, drug and alcohol abuse, crime and low educational standards became increasingly prominent in both countries as they entered periods of decline.

In summary, the United States shares many of the characteristics of former leading powers in a period of decline. The examples used were with Great Britain but Greece, Rome, Spain and the Netherlands all exhibited similar characteristics in their stages of decline. Although not cast in stone, reversing decline in a former leading power is very difficult. No nation has been able to reverse its slide from preeminence.

> 'There will have to be less emphasis on equality of opportunity, and more on equality of condition. The traditional goals of absolute freedom and maximum economic abundance will have to be modified in the more intricate equilibrium of a society that accepts the limits of human possibility and strives for the greatest possible measure of justice and equality. It will not be easy. Yet, sooner or later, the American people will have no alternative but to attempt it.'
> *America In Our Time*, Hodgson

Societies develop myths and beliefs to develop a workable mindset for their society. The United States is part of the Western tradition and shares numerous similarities with Europe. Specifically, the United States has obtained many of its institutions and law from Great Britain. Anglo-Saxon countries, including the United States, share many similarities.

However, given America's geography and distance from the Old World, Americans have developed a distinct set of ideas to deal with its environment. Americans developed rugged individualism and a frontier mentality as workable myths to organize its society. The expansive geography of the United States is likely to have provided this attitude. Americans have room for expansion. Unlike Europe, much of it highly populated, the United States has vast areas of land for inhabitation.

America, having a large market and vast resources, allowed it to take advantage of scales of economy offered by mass production. A long period of prosperity resulted in intolerance toward poverty. Government assistance ran counter to the idea of individual responsibility. Also, prosperity encouraged Americans to develop optimism as a creed. The belief that Americans can achieve anything is also the result of a long period of economic prosperity.

However, the world political economy has changed and along with it the requirements for success. Nations that are more communitarian and integrative appear to have the edge in the 21st century. Japan is an example of a successful nation that emphasizes cohesiveness and frugalness in its society.

In order to solve fundamental problems Americans will need to change these cherished beliefs. It is unlikely that wholesales change will result. Rather incremental change is likely where Americans slowly adapt to the more successful ways of other countries. It will be difficult for many Americans to make the transition.

The most likely response in the United States will be the cyclical return to a more communitarian society. Historically, the coming of age of a new generation creates demand for a significant change in how society is organized. The current period of conservatism is likely to end with the 2004 presidential election bringing this era that began in 1968 to a close (just as the election of Richard Nixon in 1968 brought to a close the liberal era that began in 1932).

For this reason, Democrats will likely dominate politics for thirty-two or thirty-six years after 2004 much as Republicans dominated during the previous political period. American society will move toward a more regulated society in both the social and economic realms. Laissez-faire attitudes will go out of favor as New Deal governance increasingly is demanded. Both Democrats and Republicans will need to change.

National liberals (FDR, Truman and Johnson) accomplished most of the major public policy of the 20th century by expanding personal liberty and providing economic security. Had New Deal-vital center democrats succeeded in completing the policies of the 1960s the dramatic increase in inequality might not have occurred. The liberal establishment came closest to the cooperative society that parallels Japan and Germany. This type of governance might be a framework for the 21st century.

Nonetheless, Americans seem to have permanently turned away from the liberal experiment started under Franklin Roosevelt and continued through Lyndon Johnson. The 1932-1968 liberal years were born out of exceptional times that demanded greater cooperation: the Great Depression, World War II and Cold War. Without a shock to America significant change is unlikely. Despite the appearance of adaptability, American culture is quite resistant to change and is the oldest democracy with institutions dating to the 18th century.

> 'The United States may not be a 'loser' in the face of global changes, as many desperate societies in the developing world will be, but because of its social and economic structure it could be less than a clear 'winner.' While an impressive array of American individuals, companies, banks, investors, and think tanks are scrambling to prepare for the twenty-first century, the United States as a whole is not and indeed cannot, without becoming a different kind of country.'
> *Preparing for the 21st Century*, Kennedy

The United States seems to be reaching a social, economic and political equilibrium where economic growth is slower and inequality much higher. Most Americans accept more plentiful but lower paid jobs while reelecting candidates from the two major political parties. A majority of Americans are suburbanized and are insulated from many of the nation's problems. World events are even further removed. The events of the Sixties and Seventies (Vietnam, Watergate and Oil Embargo) have not raised significant questions in the minds of most Americans.

Traditionally, America has been viewed as a youthful nation. Compared to the median age of other developed nations the United States is youthful. However, in terms of institutions and law America is the oldest democracy. Furthermore, the founding fathers designed American government to be fragmented with weak central authority in order to prevent monarchy. Separation of powers, strong state rights and fragmented municipal governance ensures that power is devolved. This political system provides a stable and firm foundation that is hard to undermine.

Unfortunately, this institutional stability prevents real change from occurring. The United States is unlikely to undergo fundamental change without a real jar to its system. The last great upheaval occurred during the Great Depression when Americans decided to grant government a greater role in society. Since, there has been no issue that has galvanized the citizens of the United States. Even the 1960s did not result in fundamental change in American institutions. The result will likely be inaction where competing factions compromise and generate piecemeal action that satisfies most to a certain degree.

The most likely shock to the world political system will be an over-supply of production creating a severe imbalance with laissez-faire capitalism. Open markets and free trade would worsen the situation as nations attempt to prop up their own currencies but that undermines other nations doing the same. This situation is similar to what happened during the 1997 Asian crisis and the Great Depression. A future scenario is likely considering the growing surplus of supply.

Ironically, the crisis in the United States is likely to be less severe than in industrializing Asia and Europe. Asia has more manufacturing to be adversely affected by a surplus in the world's production of goods. Europe has maintained more of its high wage jobs and will likely be affected more during an economic downturn. As a result, the coming economic downturn will not likely generate the political upheaval in the United States as it will in other nations.

An analogy can be made with Great Britain. Great Britain weathered the Great Depression better than most countries. Conversely, the United States experienced a considerable drop in production. The United States had more manufacturing to lose than Great Britain. Currently, Japan is the leader in high-value manufacturing while the United States has deindustrialized. The fact that Japan has a prolonged slump while the United States has fared better does not bode well for America's future. It is an indication that the United States is a declining power that has lost its preeminence in manufacturing while Japan is an ascending power with much manufacturing ability.

The reign of laissez-faire capitalism will come to an end when the United States can no longer be able to afford to buy the world's surplus goods that have been keeping the system in relative balance. As American trade deficits become unmanageable foreigners will lose confidence in the dollar and America's ability to borrow to buy will significantly be diminished.

A prolonged period of deflationary cost cutting will create a cycle of diminishing purchasing power (similar to how Keynes described the Great Depression). The world will come out of this crisis when Asian wages increase allowing more goods to be purchased. This will recreate a balance between supply and demand. Nonetheless, as a result of these events, laissez-faire capitalism will be largely discredited.

This scenario is hardly mentioned among America's elites. Instead a sunny outlook is championed that America has a New Economy and is destined to lead in the 21st century. Unfortunately, history and the world political economy do not support this confidence. It is likely that America's decline will continue considering the probable outcomes of the next economic downturn.

However, this will create discontent in the United States when events do not confirm beliefs of American exceptionality. National moods will oscillate between contentment and alarm generating a volatile political body. These swings in attitude will likely continue as Americans adjust to their diminished role in the world political economy.

An honest and powerful national response is unlikely. Most likely, Americans will come to grips with long-term decline on an individual basis. For example, one small city newspaper in upstate New York asks 'Is the sun setting on the U.S. empire?' comparing the United States with Great Britain at the turn of the early 20th century ('The 21st century tees off,' *Press & Sun-Bulletin*, August 9, 1998). Other Americans will raise similar questions.

II

Measuring Wealth: Efficiency and Equality

> 'The well-being of the economy is a lot like the well-being of an individual. My happiness depends almost entirely on a few important things, like work, love and health, and everything else is not really worth worrying about.' *The Age of Diminished Expectations*, Krugman

Many different characteristics determine the wealth of a nation: culture, politics, economics and geography are some important factors. Sometimes, a nation is known for a particular strength. Germany is known for engineering, Italy for design, France for fashion and Great Britain for international finance.

However, to a large degree, economic wealth determines a nation's influence in the world political economy. The Soviet Union was able to exert power based on military strength for a period of time. Yet, the lack of economic power undermined its longevity. Conversely, Japan has arisen with only limited armed forces. Throughout history, wealth has been the determining factor in societies that have risen to leading power.

Furthermore, all parts of a society are interconnected. Wealth (or the lack of it) in one sector of society influences other sectors. Economic wealth provides the foundation for social, political and cultural strength. Throughout history the affluent that have accumulated wealth have dispersed money for other signs of cultural attainment: art, museums, public works and education. The social welfare state increasingly performs this function providing money for research universities, space programs and foreign aid.

Many economic statistics exist to measure economic wealth. Some statistics measure short-term economic performance in specific sectors of the economy (e.g. economic leading indicators). Others attempt to measure the long-term performance of the total economy. These broad long-term measures of economic performance are the most useful for determining national wealth. Specifically, what economic statistics should be used to measure the long-term performance of the total economy?

The natural world can illuminate useful measurements for understanding human society. Many seemingly random events in the natural world follow a predictable pattern called a normal curve. Specifically, a wide variety of populations show similarities in the distribution of characteristics around an average. Human society is not an exception. Even in the complexity of nation-states humans still operate within natural laws and are likely to exhibit similar patterns.

Considering the importance of the distribution of characteristics around an average in the natural world what economic statistics correlate with these two measurements? Two statistics measure the distribution and average of national economic wealth: the Gini ratio and productivity. Basically, these two statistics measure the standard of living of a nation and how fully its citizens share in this wealth. Economics is complex with many theories and approaches. Yet, these two measures encapsulate the large issues of national wealth.

1. Efficiency: Productivity

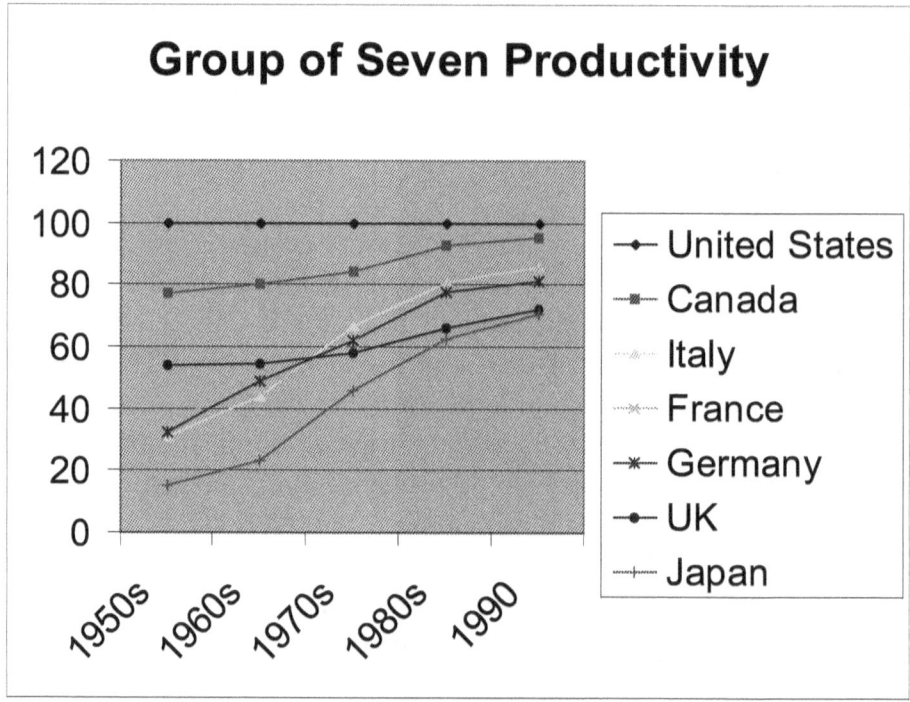

Group of Seven Productivity

Legend: United States, Canada, Italy, France, Germany, UK, Japan

OECD

> 'Productivity isn't everything, but in the long run it is almost every-
> thing. A country's ability to improve its standard of living over time
> depends almost entirely on its ability to raise its output per worker
> (productivity).' *The Age of Diminished Expectations*, Krugman

The most important factor in determining a nation's position in the
world political economy is the overall standard of living. Many different
statistics measure standard of living. Per capita GNP (gross national

product) has been one important statistic. Per capital GDP (gross domestic product) is sometimes viewed as a more accurate measure of wealth due to differences in what is included in wealth. Differences also exist between average and median income. In a nation like the United States where wealth is concentrated at the top median income is a more accurate measure of wealth. Median wealth divides wage earners equally above and below the average wage earner reducing the bias of low or high earners.

Underlying all statistical measures for standard of living is productivity. Productivity is measured as output per person. In the long run, productivity and standard of living are essentially the same. They may diverge in the short run but closely parallel each other over a long period of time. In fact, productivity determines standard of living. No other measure is so important in determining national wealth.

Differences exist in productivity statistics. The most inclusive productivity statistic is multifactorate productivity that includes all economic activity in an economy. This is very difficult to measure and differences between economists exist as to what is the best method to obtain this statistic. For example, software was reclassified as an investment increasing productivity statistics during the 1990s. Labor productivity is more easily calculated.

Productivity statistics fluctuate significantly from quarter to quarter. It is not uncommon for productivity to dramatically differ from one year to the next. The general trend is for the rate of productivity to increase during recoveries and decrease during recessions. To obtain an accurate measure of long-term productivity economists use the beginning and endpoint of a business cycle for measurement. Otherwise, productivity figures can be distorted.

Furthermore, productivity can be difficult to compare between nations. Different nations use different means to derive productivity statistics. Obtaining productivity figures is difficult. For that reason per capita GDP is the most readily available statistic for comparing standard of living between nations. One may need to consult more technical bulletins to get up-to-date productivity statistics.

Interestingly, productivity differs between different regions even within the same nation. Traditionally, the industrial Northeast has had substantially higher costs of living than the American South. For example, wages continue to remain much higher in New Jersey than in Mississippi even though the cost of living is higher in New Jersey. It would seem that the higher cost of living in New Jersey would mean residents would be poorer than those in Mississippi with a lower cost of living.

Yet, it is because productivity is higher in New Jersey that residents are better off than in Mississippi. The higher cost of living is more than offset by the higher levels of productivity. Therefore, it does not matter that the cost of living is lower in Mississippi because productivity is even lower.

This example illuminates the importance of productivity in maintaining a high standard of living. The search by American corporations for cheap labor may prove to be futile as the key is not necessarily low cost but high productivity. Germany is an example of a nation with high labor costs but with high productivity. Germany can afford to pay its workers high wages precisely because they are so productive.

Unfortunately, American firms have succeeded in keeping wages stagnant but have not matched the productivity gains of many of its competitors. The result will be an American workforce with cheap labor but relatively low productivity. Great Britain is an example of a former leading power that resorted to cheap labor to no avail. Labor and management have traditionally been adversarial with British management looking for financial ways to cut costs. However, investment and wages were short-changed with the result that Great Britain ranked 16th in wages at the turn of the 20th century.

The leading industrial nations are collectively named the Group of Seven (Russia joining created the Group of Eight). These nations have the highest level of economic development and are ranked at the top in terms of productivity. Therefore, it is useful to look at the productivity figures for these nations in order to understand the direction that other nations must measure up to in order to effectively compete.

The Group of Seven includes the major industrial nations: Canada, France, Germany, Italy, Japan, the United Kingdom and United States. After World War II the productivity rate for the United States, Japan and Western Europe was robust. Western Europe (France, West Germany and Italy) saw rapid rebuilding of their economies. However, the most dramatic recovery was in Japan. Japan experienced the greatest increase in productivity gains. During the 1960s growth rates were in the double digits.

However, the rate of productivity decreased in all of these nations after the 1973–74 recession. Even Japan experienced a significant decrease in productivity. Surprisingly, the most significant drop occurred in the United States. The rate of productivity in the United States decreased from a historical rate of 2.3% to 1.1% after 1973.

A plausible explanation for the productivity rate after the 1973 slow-down is the introduction of flexible manufacturing combined with rising energy prices. OPEC dramatically increased oil prices while the price for raw materials increased. Ironically, those nations that relied most heavily on the import of raw materials (Japan and Western Europe) fared better than the United States.

At the same time, a new type of manufacturing based on rapid product changes developed. Japan and Europe were best suited to take advantage of this change. The American system of mass manufacturing that relied on relatively few product changes fared poorly. Flexible manufacturing used just-in-time inventory avoiding the build-up of inventory and waste common in the mass production system of the United States.

However, flexible manufacturing did not improve productivity until several decades later. It appears that it takes time for manufacturers to learn how to use new technology. For example, the effects of electricity on productivity did not appear until several decades after being introduced. It appears that the same was true of flexible manufacturing. The microchip, computerization and Internet were new technologies that did not have an immediate impact as productivity remained low throughout the 1970s, 1980s and early 1990s when these technologies were introduced.

Since 1996, productivity has remained higher than in the last two decades after the 1973 slowdown. It appears that businesspeople are figuring out how to effectively use new technology. A convergence of technologies has contributed to this increased level of productivity. Furthermore, changes in productivity statistics in the United States to account for software purchases have improved productivity statistics during the 1990s.

Initially, gains in productivity were concentrated in computers. However, information technology usage is spreading. It is likely that productivity gains will spread to other areas of business. Unfortunately, American investment in high technology has tended to be in low value areas such as distribution, retail and data processing.

Furthermore, even though productivity growth rates have increased in the United States other nations are not standing still. The relative slow growth in productivity of the United States will likely remain. Already, Asia and Europe are leaders in various information technologies. The United States continues to lose manufacturing to Asian firms while Europe surges ahead in wireless technology using a universally accepted GSM standard.

The rapid increase of the stock market is not indicative of long-term improvements in productivity relative to other nations. The rapid increase in the value of the stock market during the 1990s is the combination of improved productivity *and* speculation. It is important to remember that profitability and productivity are different. It is also important to remember that stock markets have increased in value in a number of nations.

An interesting exception is the stagnation of Japan's stock market that collapsed in 1989. Since Japan's stock market bubble the Japanese economy has stagnated. For the time being, Japan's model of capitalism seems to have faded. Yet, it is important to remember that Japan continues to produce world-class products that are in high demand across the globe. The United States continues to run huge trade deficits with Japan. This continuing and large trade deficit is an indication that the United States does not produce what others want to buy.

Cost cutting has played a major role in the improved profitability of American firms. Even though European firms have begun to cut labor costs most have not gone to the massive layoffs that occurred in the United States. Japan is edging toward making performance more important and seniority less influential in promotions. However, manufacturing has remained robust in Japan while the United States continues to lose manufacturing ability.

It appears that Japan has replaced the United States as manufacturer while the United States has replaced Great Britain as a financier. The Great Depression hit the United States with a severity greater than many other nations because it had more manufacturing to lose. Ironically, Great Britain's ability to survive this catastrophe better than most nations was a sign of long-term weakness in manufacturing. World War II proved that the United States was a sleeping giant that could quickly produce the arsenal of democracy. Britain's relatively mild depression was a mirage of temporary success.

The United States is in a similar position today with less industry to lose than Japan. The irony is that America's robust economy at the turn of the 20th century is a sign of long-term weakness not strength. Conversely, Japan's economic slump is a sign of long-term strength not weakness.

The result may be hollowed out companies that will be unable to expand market share. American firms increasingly outsource manufacturing retaining only a small core of workers. In time, foreign manufacturers have created their own brands competing against the

American firms they once produced for. Productivity gains are most easily obtained in manufacturing due to falling costs per unit. Since the United States has less manufacturing productivity gains will be harder to obtain.

The next recession could be severe as there is a growing surplus of production worldwide. As mentioned, Asia's 1997 crisis was in part created by the growing surplus of manufacturing in this region. Asia had more productive capacity to lose. The result of this growing manufacturing surplus and falling prices will be a significant downturn that could lead to depression in some parts of the world. Asia will be hardest hit (due to the concentration of manufacturing) with European unemployment remaining high. The United States will experience the mildest economic downturn (however, as mentioned, as a sign of weakness rather than strength).

It is likely that the stock market will either decline or stagnate for a long period of time in the United States as productivity gains moderate and the effect of foreign competition intensifies. Many boomers and other Americans who have relied on an increasing stock market for savings will find themselves relatively poor. This will further dampen demand and depress wages and economic growth. This economic stagnation could continue for a period of time lasting for a decade or more. Previous periods of stock market peaks have been followed by several decades of stagnant stock prices (e.g. 1901, 1929 and 1966). It is likely that the rapid rise in the stock market starting in 1982 will come to a close in the first decade of the 21st century.

For those Americans that are relatively debt free and employed in secure occupations this prolonged period of economic stagnation will be relatively minor. However, those with few savings and high debt could experience considerable problems. Some will fall into poverty and experience permanent setbacks. Although the severe deprivation of the Great Depression will not return many will experience stagnant or declining wages for a prolonged period of time. Many Americans (and not all poor) will be ill prepared for this change in economic circumstances. It is important for Americans to remember that this period of economic stagnation (and retraction) will exist for a period of time and to be prepared for this.

2. Equality: Gini ratio

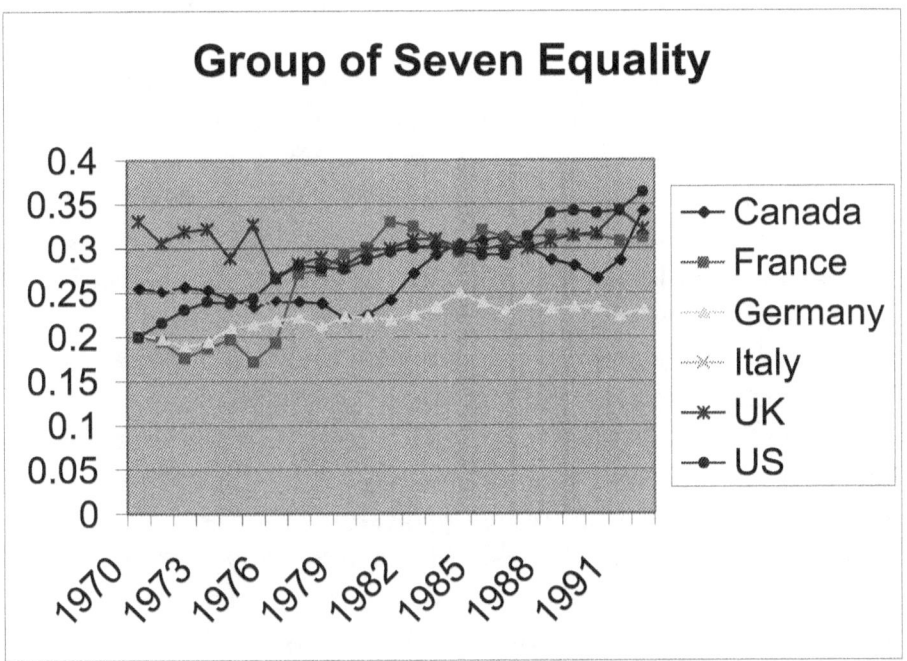

Created Unequal, Galbraith

The wealth of a nation is fundamentally measured not just by the amount of wealth but how fully its citizens share in the wealth. Wealth distribution can be measured by several different statistics. Most create a ratio using a certain percentage of wage earners at the top and bottom.

The Gini ratio is one particular statistic that measures wealth distribution. The Gini ratio measures the difference between the top 20 percent of wage earners with the bottom 20 percent producing a ratio between zero and one. A Gini ratio of zero indicates perfect equality while one indicates perfect inequality.

The major pattern of equality in the world is for industrialized nations to have the highest equality (and highest efficiency) while poor nations have the lowest equality (and lowest efficiency). The poorest nations have large percentages of its population in poverty while a small elite often rule by force. The middle class is small and precarious. It appears that industrialization generates relatively larger middle classes and less poverty.

Equality among the Group of Seven has remained relatively stable over the last thirty years. As mentioned, most of these leading industrial nations have high levels of equality. Rapid growth after World War II coincided with growing equality for most industrialized nations. Many experienced increased levels of equality and expanded rights and benefits for the middle class. In the United States, Lyndon Johnson expanded on the New Deal with the Great Society Program. In the United States, the elderly have the lowest rates of poverty largely due to social welfare programs (e.g. Social Security and Medicare).

However, since the economic slowdown in the early 1970s, the Anglo-Saxon nations have experienced growing inequality. The most dramatic increase occurred in the United States. Previously, the United States had one of the largest middle classes in the world and a standard of living that was the envy of the world. This rapidly began to change when the United States began to lose supremacy in mass manufacturing.

The similarity in growing inequality of all Anglo-Saxon nations points to a problem in the underlying structure of these nations. Australia, New Zealand, Canada, Great Britain and the United States (all English-speaking countries with similar lineages) have experienced the slowest growth rates with the greatest increase in inequality. It is likely that these nations share structural characteristics that contribute to the wealth patterns of these nations.

Anglo-Saxon nations share individualistic societies that, to different degrees, have increasingly relied on finance to generate profits. Deindustrialization has advanced furthest in these nations. New Zealand has gone furthest in deregulating its economy. Anglo-Saxon nations share the tendency to rely on free markets to promote investment and industry. Outside of English-speaking nations, belief in the free market is muted. Even continental Europe is suspicious of Anglo-Saxon laissez-faire capitalism.

Most importantly, the one nation that stands out in worsening inequality is the United States. Since the mid-1970s, inequality considerably increased in the United States. Currently, the United States has the highest inequality of any industrialized nation (even higher than Great Britain that has a system of class division). This is a drastic about face from America's history of high equality and large middle class.

Social historian Alex de Tocqueville commented on the equality of condition of Americans compared to Europeans in his seminal work *Democracy in America*. As recently as the 1970s, equality had not increased since the 18th century and was average in comparison to other developed nations. However, during the late 1970s, the United States developed the highest inequality in the developed world.

President Bill Clinton speaking in reference to the 1996 Census Bureau's income statistics said 'America's middle class, no longer forgotten, is rising fast.' However, the best-selling novel *Bonfire of the Vanities* written by Tom Wolfe during the 1980s more accurately portrayed America: as a nation of division with those at the top pulling away from those at the bottom. Inequality significantly increased under both Ronald Reagan in the 1980s and Bill Clinton in the 1990s.

Some refute the statistics saying that social mobility is greater in the United States than other developed nations. However, evidence finds that social mobility is average for Americans in the middle and actually lower for those at the very bottom and top in comparison to other industrial nations. Most middle class Americans have opportunities no better or worse (at the turn of the 21st century) than middle class citizens in other industrial nations. However, getting out of poverty is more difficult in the United States than in any other industrialized nation. Also, getting into the upper class appears more difficult in the United States.

United States Equality (darker counties more unequal)

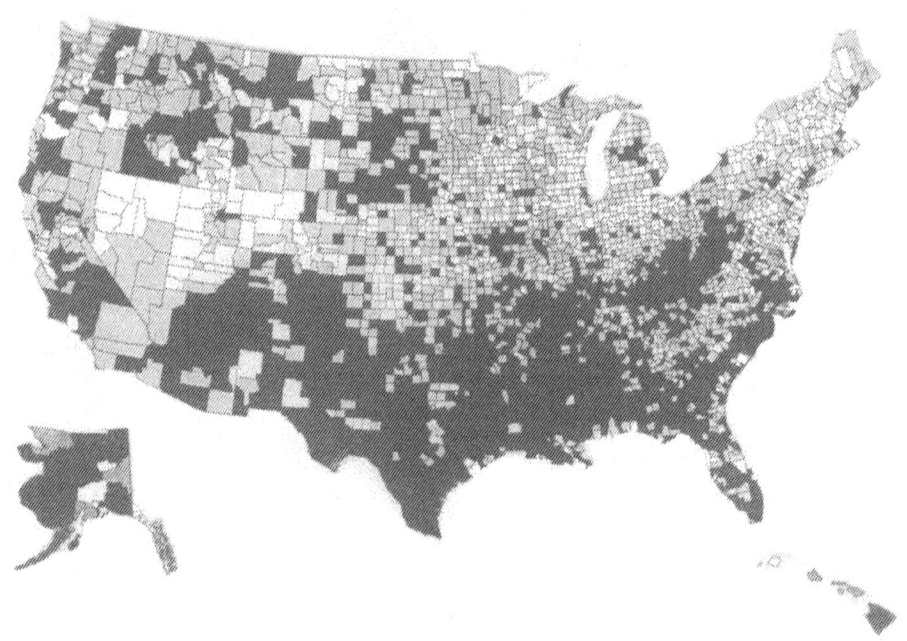

'Mapping income inequality,' USA Today, September 20, 1996

Research done by *USA Today* indicates that inequality increased in every region and group between 1980 and 1996. Furthermore, inequality grew within all groups: education levels (including college graduates), race, gender and generations.

Historically, the South and Southwest have had the highest inequality bearing the legacy of racial segregation. Even with rapid growth since the 1970s the South and Southwest became even more unequal. However, states that experienced the most significant increases in inequality had high levels of manufacturing. As the United States deindustrialized, these industrialized states experienced rapid increases in inequality. Ironically, the state that experienced the least amount of increasing inequality was Mississippi. It appears that the labor structure of the United States has become more like the South.

Racial segregation remains an important factor in American society. However, class supersedes race as a dividing line. Again, deindustrialization has left behind many minorities in the inner cities that had previously been employed in manufacturing. However, at the same time the civil rights movement has greatly accelerated the entry of minorities into previously closed professional occupations. As a result, a contradiction has arisen in the race issue. *Simultaneously*, African-Americans have become better and worse-off than in previous decades. The dividing line is class. Those minorities with access to better-paying occupations have fared better. Those without this access have fared poorly.

The women's movement has affected gender much like the civil rights movement. Women who have been able to take advantage of the opening of professions to women have done well. However, many women in formerly good-paying manufacturing occupations have had to take lower paying jobs in services. Even though the pay gap has decreased between men and women this is due more to the salaries of blue-collar men falling rather than women's rising. The women's movement, much like the civil rights movements, has class superseding gender as the major dividing line.

Much was made of the generation gap during the 1960s. However, it was the inequality in social and economic capital afterwards that had the most impact. During the latter part of the 20th century twelve times the amount of public assistance was provided to the elderly than the young. Social Security for the elderly takes up far more of the Federal budget than welfare for young mothers. Culturally, American society has revolved around the baby boomer generation (and now their children). Generations outside these groups have tended to be excluded in national discussions.

The overriding influence on equality in the United States is class. Most surprisingly, for a nation with the highest inequality in the industrial world, many Americans support the myth of a classless society. Supposedly, every American has an equal change at success. Effort is all that is needed. This view distorts the understanding of the United States and makes resolution of problems difficult. For example, poverty is the determining factor in whether a girl will bear a child as a teenager. Yet, American society moralizes teenage pregnancy and treats the solution as merely a failing of the individual.

One important result of growing inequality is that the United States has the smallest middle-class of any developed nation. For a nation that once prided itself as being the leading middle-class society this is quite a turnaround. Americans once prided themselves as not having the class structure of Great Britain or other European nations. This is no longer true. Ironically, many poor, working and middle-class Americans would be wealthier if they had remained in Europe.

As the rich and poor separate, the notion of a middle-class America is fading into the past. For example, in industry after industry, the market is bifurcating. One-third of Americans are stuck in jobs paying less than $15,000 a year (for example, read 'Two-tier marketing,' *Business Week,* March 17, 1997). To make matters worse, the United States is the only industrialized nation among sixty-three that has no form of guaranteed minimum income.

Throughout history, societies that have been leading powers but experienced both increasing inequality and declining economic prosperity, have been in the early stages of decline. It is very likely that this is the case of the United States. This would be a significant and long-lasting result of the deindustrialization of the United States.

Great Britain experienced declining fortunes in its industry at the turn of the 20th century. Class differences hardened and generated a constant source of conflict for over a century. Class has overridden many issues in British society. It is said that one dies in the class that one is born. In other words, there is little social mobility.

Is the United States creating a similar social structure based on class? Events seem to support this belief. The United States has the highest inequality of the developed world. No leading power that entered the first stages of imperial decline has been able to reverse this situation. A nation of large differences between the poor and wealthy will likely remain in the United States and for a long period of time. It is not unthinkable that class will be the defining feature of the United States for the next century or more. This scenario came true for Great Britain and will likely come true for the United States.

3. Equality & Efficiency: A Trade-off?

THE FULFILLMENT CURVE

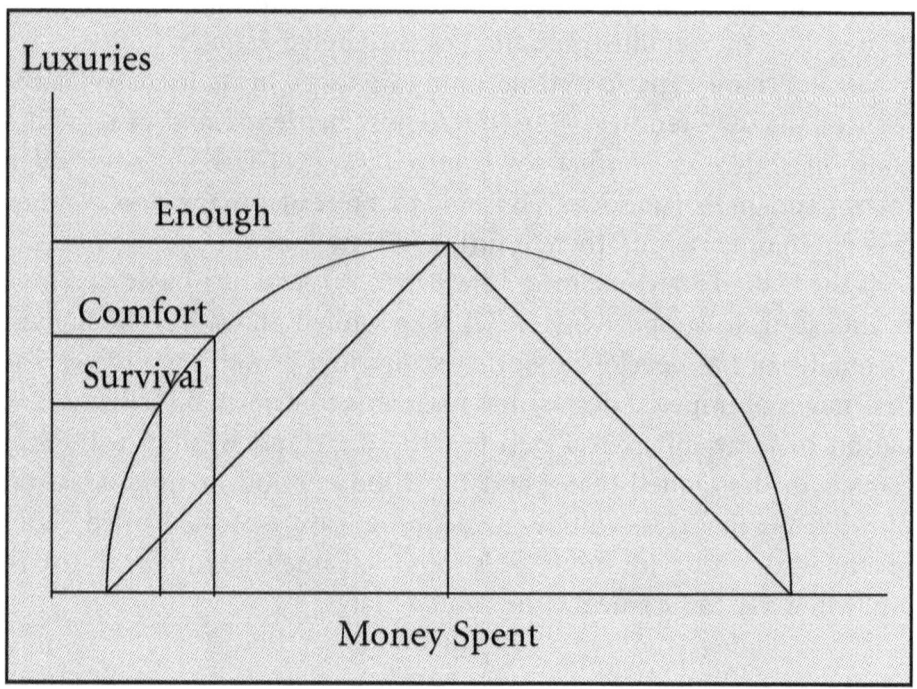

Your Money or Your Life, Dominguez & Robin

'Americans fundamentally understand democracy to mean competition.

> The American word satisfaction, which has its origin in the Latin word satis (enough), has unfortunately lost its original meaning. The only way to attain freedom is to let something be enough instead of always demanding more.
>
> Freedom like money seeks to expand if no outside forces interfere. But an expansion of freedom paradoxically yields not more but less freedom. In Aristotle's view, human values are not something one-dimensional that can be attained with the simple equation "more=better." Rather, they are located in a median position between two extremes (=nonvalues). Once this high point is reached, there is no increase in value, only a renewed decline into the other extreme.'
> *Society on the Run*, Peters

The advent of agriculture several thousand years ago brought a period of increasing inequality to the world. Whereas a state of relative equality appears to have existed before the advent of agriculture, urbanization that resulted from the ability to amass surplus food generated growing differences between the common person and elite. This situation continued until the Industrial Revolution.

Surprisingly, the Industrial Revolution reversed this trend of inequality. The growing prosperity of the middle class resulted from the need for a broad range of occupations such as management that industrialization demanded. The Enlightenment and French Revolution resulted from the growing affluence created by the Industrial Revolution. These movements challenged the idea that monarchies had innate power based on hereditary. The American Revolution went furthest in promoting equality.

Subsequently, most nations followed the path of democracy and granted more rights to growing middle classes in the industrialized nations. Nations with high productivity are industrialized and have high equality. Europe, Japan and United States (until recently) all are highly industrialized, have large middle classes and are relatively prosperous. In other words, affluent nations are both relatively efficient and equal.

Conversely, the poorest nations have both low equality and low efficiency. These nations have not industrialized and rely on a much larger proportion of its population working in agriculture. Middle classes are small or virtually nonexistent. In addition, productivity is low. Brazil has been an example of a nation with a small ruling elite with many poor. Much of the surrounding area in Latin America exhibits ruling elites that control many poor. Central America often is a hot spot for conflict. Sub-Sahara Africa shares many of the similarities of highly unequal and unjust societies. Again, many work in agriculture for subsistence.

Some in the United States see the high inequality as a necessary condition for the successful motivation of its citizens. However, the situation of Africa, Latin America and Middle East do not support this belief. These regions have both low equality and low productivity. Only those nations with high equality have high efficiency. The perceived trade-off between equality and efficiency may not exist.

Interestingly, only societies that are in the declining stages of their history have experienced growing inequality. Societies at the peak of their power from Greece onwards have had influential middle-classes. Considering the fact that the United States has the highest inequality in the industrialized world after a long period of low inequality does not bode well for this nation.

During the two centuries after the American Revolution the United States experienced both fast growth and high equality. Relative to societies in Europe that grew out of the monarchic system of rule Americans had a large middle class. Industrialization provided rapid growth for the young growing nation. For example, Chicago grew from a small population in 1850 to many times its size at the turn of the 20th century.

Not until productivity growth rates significantly slowed after 1973 did inequality increase in the United States. Starting in the late 1970s the United States developed increasing inequality and a growing and permanent under-class (the only multigeneration underclass in the developed world). The decrease in both equality and efficiency may not be a coincidence.

As the increase in wealth slows, individuals look for ways to maintain previous levels of increasing wealth. If the pie is not expanding then one alternative solution is to change the way the pie is sliced. Americans at the top of the socio-economic spectrum appear to have found ways to increase their wealth relative to other Americans. Indeed, this is what has happened at the end of the 20th century.

Great Britain at the turn of the 19th century found their society in a similar predicament. British manufacturing lost competitiveness relative to American and German manufacturers. British manufacturing declined resulting in the increasing impoverishment of the working class in blue-collar cities like Liverpool, Manchester and Birmingham, England. The elite in Great Britain turned to finance and services to sustain revenues. As a result, the fortunes of the working class and elite hardened class differences.

Likewise, finance and services hold the attention of affluent Americans that have looked to areas to obtain high levels of return on capital. Ironically, the push for high short-term profitability that benefits the upper class hurts the working class by lowering wages and limiting investment for the long term.

Conversely, Japan and Germany, leaders in productivity exhibit high equality. As these nations emerged from the ashes of World War II the middle classes grew proportionally. Wealth did not collect in the hands of the few. The high inequality that some in the United States claim is necessary for motivating citizens did not exist in these successful nations.

One reason may be that high equality spreads wealth throughout society generating purchasing power for the middle and lower classes.

Another is that large differences in wealth create market inefficiencies by overrewarding individuals at the top. Most importantly, large differences in wealth undermine the principles of democracy and create alienation among the lower classes. One does not need to listen to British punk rock to realize the negative effects of an alienated working class.

Finally, maintaining a balance between equality and efficiency may contribute to general happiness. Happiness rises steeply with economic development until you reach the level of Ireland. Beyond that, there is hardly any relationship between prosperity and happiness. Happiness occurs when desires and accomplishments are congruent. The key is being content with what you can actually attain. For example, Scandinavians score highest on the happiness scale because they are small, manageable, homogeneous and prosperous nations, where life is predictable (for example, read 'Get happy,' *Maclean's*, September 16, 1996).

Sources of Economic Statistics

Computerization and the Internet allow the generation of numerous economic statistics. Most are familiar with some of the many statistics provided at regular intervals by different institutions (e.g. unemployment figures). It is difficult to decipher the many and sometimes conflicting statistics. However, even though different statistics exist for the same measurement, there is general agreement on a reasonable range of results. Results from some institutions are more trusted than others.

Productivity figures are hard to obtain and difficult to compare between nations. As mentioned, deriving multifactorate productivity is more difficult than labor productivity. Determining multifactorate productivity involves obtaining accurate measurement of economic output in all areas of the economy. Comparison between nations is even more difficult due to differences in hours worked, differences in measurements and other factors.

Gini ratio statistics (or similar measurements of equality) are also difficult to obtain. The impact of smaller family size, measuring income from non-cash sources and determining quality of life improvements generate differences among economists as to what is the appropriate level of equality. Technical periodicals and bulletins may need to be referenced for some nations.

Most industrial nations maintain economic statistics through a particular bureau or ministry. For example, the Census Bureau and Department of Labor Statistics in the United States provide many economic statistics. Statistics Canada provides statistical information for Canada. Other nations have their own agencies disseminating economic statistics.

Major international organizations maintain statistics. The Organization for Economic Cooperation and Development (OECD), International Monetary Fund (IMF) and World Bank are major providers of a wide variety of economic statistics. For instance, *OECD in Figures* is one informative yearbook.

Finally, private organizations maintain statistics. The *Economist* produces an annual compilation of statistics as well as periodic articles on economic statistics. The Economic Policy Institute, a Washington think tank, produces a yearly report titled *The State of Working America.* While the *Economist* takes a favorable view toward laissez-faire capitalism the Economic Policy Institute tends to question this framework. It is important to consider these biases.

III

Creating Wealth: Cooperative Investment in Competitive Manufacturing

Wealth has greatly increased since the inception of the Industrial Revolution. This expansion in wealth is not restricted to the simple accumulation of money. All areas of life have been affected. For example, the top speed of humans depended on the speed of a horse. The Industrial Revolution greatly advanced this to where at the turn of the 20th century trains approached 100 miles per hour. Similar advances were made in a wide array of areas in life.

The advancement in technology has occurred throughout human history. The Industrial Revolution simply magnified and condensed the period and intensity of change. Since agriculture was developed human society has been on an accelerated path of development. Cities only came into being several thousand years ago. This is a very short time frame when considering the long expanse of human existence.

Technology is the crucial development that has allowed human society to advance. The plow, wheel and steam engine among other inventions have increased the output per person (productivity) allowing the standard of living to increase for human society. Only by increasing the output per person has the ability to create surplus wealth occurred. The manipulation and development of tools to change the environment through technology changed human productivity.

Since the capitalist market evolved in the 13th century key inventions developed by a particular nation-state have given this nation the ability to dominate the world political economy. This society was able to take advantage of a developing technology because a constellation of resources was organized most effectively to take advantage of the new technology.

From the 1930s through 1960s New York City and the surrounding area was able to capitalize on the technological invention of the electric motor. New York's success helped propel the United States to the world's leading power. This region produced a significant proportion of the world's manufactured goods during and after World War II. Not coincidentally, New York City was chosen as the headquarters for the United Nation's after World War II. Many factors played a role in the dominance of the New York City region: the success of America's mass manufacturing, an effective political system and good geographical location. The interaction between variables is complex. It was not certain that New York City and the surrounding region would lead the world's political economy after World War II.

Similarities can be outlined in the social, political and economic structures of rising nations. What appears crucial is the investment in technology (specifically, manufacturing) by a wide array of social institutions that leads to rapid productivity gains. Rising nations are able to generate synergy between different sectors of society and technology.

1. Competitive Manufacturing

'There are those who still believe that America can move from the strongest core industrial economy in the world to essentially a service economy without losing its greatness, its dynamism, and its industrial health. I am absolutely certain we cannot. I think very few people who go into the service economy will go into what might be called high-service jobs. Far more of them will be jobs in the low-service sector.'
The Next Century, Halberstam

Some economists say that the United States needs to move into a post-industrial information economy. The post-industrialist thinking views economic history as progressing from agriculture to manufacturing to information. This view holds the imagination of many prominent American leaders. Other nations that have moved more slowly out of manufacturing are viewed as laggards.

However, the post-industrialist thinking is misplaced. America did not move out of agriculture and into manufacturing. America automated agriculture. Likewise, we are not moving from a manufacturing to a service economy. We are moving toward a hyperindustrial economy where manufacturing will complement services. If a nation loses manufacturing it will likely lose related services. Furthermore, reliance on services creates other problems.

First, manufacturing provides higher productivity gains as costs per unit falls quicker. Gains in services appear harder to achieve. Many local economies have found themselves, after losing manufacturing jobs, gaining service jobs but at lower pay. As labor moved from high-productivity manufacturing into low-productivity services, the rate of productivity declined. Wages had to fall.

Second, services tend to worsen economic inequality. Pay in services is skewed toward the top and bottom with fewer jobs paying in the middle. Although American leaders mention the growth in higher paid occupations in finance, marketing and information the growth in lower paid industries in retail, restaurant and data processing are more numerous. Manufacturing provides a better balance of jobs.

Third, the export of services does not offset the import of manufactured goods. Software and other information technology exports do not compensate for the import of manufactured goods. Great Britain, the leading world power until the early 20th century, found that its export of services could not make up for its import of manufactured goods. The United States reached this imbalance much quicker.

It is hard to remember that as recently as 1981, the United States was a net exporter of manufactured goods and remained the leader in high technology. The large trade deficits the United States accumulated only developed between 1981 and 1984. In 1986, the United States experienced a trade deficit in high technology for the first time. One reason is that networked companies have evolved that perform the design and marketing of products but outsource production to various foreign suppliers. Therefore, many imports are from American corporations and not foreign competitors.

It is not necessary to go beyond the borders of the United States to see the impact of manufacturing. The South, until recently the poorest region, had relied on agriculture for its economy. The Northeast, until recently the richest region, had the greatest concentration of manufacturing. The concentration of manufacturing in the Northeast generated high wages, growing populations and political clout. Not until the 1970s when the South lost relatively less manufacturing than the Northeast did the South regain equality with other regions.

Not all manufacturing creates equal gains. Only high-value manufacturing generates the ability to significantly increase the standard of living. Remaining in low-value manufacturing will not advance the standard of living. The success of a nation is the ability to steadily offer greater sophistication and features in its products so to be able to obtain higher prices and greater profit margins.

For example, Japan and other Asian nations started by producing inexpensive goods that were often copied from Western nations. However, Japan improved on design and features so to obtain higher value in its products. During the 1970s Japan manufactured cheap but well-made 4-cylinder automobiles that did not directly compete with larger, more expensive and profitable American cars. However, starting in the 1980s Japanese cars steadily added features and performance expanding market share and entering more profitable areas. Eventually, by the late 1980s Japan began producing luxury vehicles that competed with Lincoln and Cadillac. The Japanese automobile history is an example of one nation successfully moving up the chain in manufacturing value.

Many do not realize but the United States formulated a similar path in competing with Great Britain in the 18th and 19th centuries. During this time the United States exported raw materials and imported finished goods from Great Britain. At first, the United States copied British goods and used designs from abroad. Cheap labor was part of the success. Yet, much success was due to the innovativeness of Americans in producing increasingly valuable products. British producers complained about Americans copying British designs much as Americans complained about the Japanese copying their designs.

The technological invention that is propelling the next nation to dominance is the microchip (not information technology). The unifying purpose of the microchip will be the manipulation of information. Wireless phones, high definition television (HDTV), personal device assistants (PDAs) and other portable electronic devices rely on this technology. Healthcare and education, currently some of the most expensive services, increasingly will use similar technology to reduce costs.

In a similar manner that American mass production changed the way things were produced in the 20th century, flexible manufacturing has changed how products are produced in the 21st century. Just-in-time inventory, quality work circles and employee ownership are examples that American manufacturers have mimicked from successful flexible manufacturers in Japan and Europe.

The trend away from mass production and toward flexible production is significant. The type and quantity in a wide variety of goods has dramatically increased. The average grocery store now carries many times the number and type of items offered only several decades before. Even the menus of fast food chains have greatly increased from a few years ago.

The computerization of manufacturing is key to allowing this great variety of goods. Most companies can track product at every step in the chain of production. The same is true of services. Wal-Mart is able to track exactly where product is sold anywhere in the United States. Grocery stores through shopper's club cards can create a detailed understanding of a particular person's tastes through products scanned at the checkout.

The most sophisticated systems allow a manufacture to produce a one-of-a-kind product. Computer-integrated manufacturing (CIM) will allow a manufacturer to produce an item that will fit the tastes of one person. This is an about face from the mass production techniques of the 20th century. Automobiles can be custom made even before they are produced. Even jeans can be made to order for one person's fit and tastes. This individualized choice in products will spread from products to services such as education.

The nation that has been able to take advantage of this the most has been Japan and Europe. Japan, unable to expand geographically and without natural resources, mastered the art of miniaturization. This talent along with flexible manufacturing gave Japan an advantage in the production of increasingly small electronic components. The Asian Tigers (Hong Kong, Singapore, Taiwan and South Korea) emulated Japan's success. Finally, China encouraged manufacturing as the means to increase its standard of living. Because of China's population and geographic size this nation will likely rise to leadership in the 21st century.

The development of technology appears to occur in spurts rather than a linear fashion. Each technological revolution creates synergy from the introduction of many products and then reaches a plateau as technology matures. The Industrial Revolution was one such spurt that resulted in a flurry of inventions. The Information Revolution that started in the middle part of the 20th century created a new wave of inventions such as the computer, wireless phone, fax, Internet and a host of related technologies.

The general trend is for numerous competitors to exist early in the technological revolution as entrants attempt to cash in on the coming boom. A wide variety of products are created many of whom will have a short life span. As the gains from technology mature and profitability is reduced there is a period of consolidation where the number and kind of products becomes fewer. Eventually, new technology arrives and the process repeats itself.

The current technological revolution will mature around the year 2020. Around that time a new type of technological invention will result based on biotechnology, genetic engineering, nanotechnology and related technologies. Fuel cells powered by hydrogen will likely replace the internal combustion engine by mid century.

'Oddly, the restrictive practices that these (U.S.) administrations claimed would be detrimental to the United States have proved enormously successful for Japan. The Japanese haven't just limited imports from the United States. They have chosen certain crucial U.S. products, such as televisions and machine tools, and subsidized their own factories to make these products, then inundated the American market with them-all the while blocking similar products made in the United States from entry into Japan.

So the solution is obvious, you say: Control imports. Bring exports into better balance.

Exactly.' *America: Who Stole the Dream?*, Barlett & Steele

United States Tariffs

1821	1840	1870	1890	1910	1929	1950	1960	1970	1980	1995
45%	34%	44%	45%	42%	40%	13%	12%	10%	6%	4%

The Great American Deception, Batra

Many influential Americans believe free trade creates the greatest wealth for all nations based on David Ricardo's theory of comparative advantage. Comparative advantage argues that all nations gain from free trade. Even if a nation can produce all goods more efficiently, a nation gains from free trade. Likewise, even if a nation is less productive in all goods, a nation gains.

However, even accepting the theoretical framework of comparative advantage, the *relative* gains from free trade are unequal. In other worlds, even if all nations gain from free trade they do not gain at the same rate. American economists have focused on the absolute gains from free trade but ignored the relative differences.

Japan and other Asian nations have not adopted free trade. Japan practices a different model of trade based on protected (regulated) trade. In industry after industry, Japan has repeated a four-step trade process:

1.   Japan's Ministry of International Trade and Industry (MITA) provide low-cost loans for export industries.

2.   Japan essentially closes its markets to foreign competitors.

3.   In order to gain access to Japanese markets, American firms license vital technology to Japanese firms producing short-term profit but long-term market share loss.

4.   Japanese firms target America for exports.

Many Asian nations, most notably China, are emulating Japan's success by restricting access to its markets. China requires American companies to provide vital technology in order to gain access to China's market of 1.2 billion. However, American firms have made few inroads in China. China is industrializing and competing with foreign firms with products made in China.

Conversely, America's experience with free trade has been less favorable. Bill Clinton with many Democrats and Republicans promised that passage of the North American Free Trade Agreement (NAFTA) would create jobs and improve the United State's trade balance. It didn't happen. Passage of NAFTA has resulted in large trade deficits with both Canada and Mexico where once we had trade surpluses. Some economists say that America's huge trade deficit is a sign of American strength in purchasing power and weakness abroad. However, an inability to sell goods to other nations is indicative of an inability to compete.

A likely consequence of America's continuing trade deficit will be a crisis of confidence in the dollar sometime during the first decades of the 21st century. Foreign nations will subsidize America's trade deficit if foreigners remain confident about the United States. However, any weakness on the part of the United States can trigger a selling of dollars leading to a currency crisis. Some argue that the size of the United States will prevent such a crisis. However, experience with Brazil and Mexico indicates that this is not the case. The United States is only prolonging a currency crisis in the future by delaying reducing the trade deficit.

> 'What encourages domestic rivalry is competitive protectionism, which the United States followed until the 1930s. When a large number of companies, secure behind tariff walls, struggle against each other to attract customers at home, then the state policy may be called competitive protectionism.
>
> America abandoned its winning formula and switched to what may be called monopolistic free trade, where mergers at home create regional monopolies, which are then exposed to foreign rivals. This is a recipe for self-destruction.' *The Great American Deception*, Batra

Americans (rightly so) are concerned that regulated trade could lead to economic inefficiency. However, competition within a nation determines competitiveness more than competition between nations. For much of American history tariffs were successfully used to protect manufacturing in the United States without hindering competitiveness because domestic competition between American firms remained intense maintaining high productivity.

Likewise, Japan has thrived with protection. Japanese institutions regulating trade insisted that Japan's protected industries become competitive. China is following a similar path by divesting state monopolies and requiring them to become efficient while limiting foreign competition.

Protected economies like the former Soviet Union have failed. Industry subsidies in nations like Brazil never worked. The difference is the lack of domestic competition. Industries in these nations never became competitive. In a similar manner, Great Britain's attempt to nationalize industries resulted primarily in reducing competition.

In the United States, antimonopoly laws have served the purpose of maintaining healthy competition. However, recent administrations have allowed mergers and acquisitions at record levels throughout the 1980s and 1990s. In declining industries, mergers and acquisitions have had the effect of reducing competition rather than improving productivity.

2. Cooperative Investment

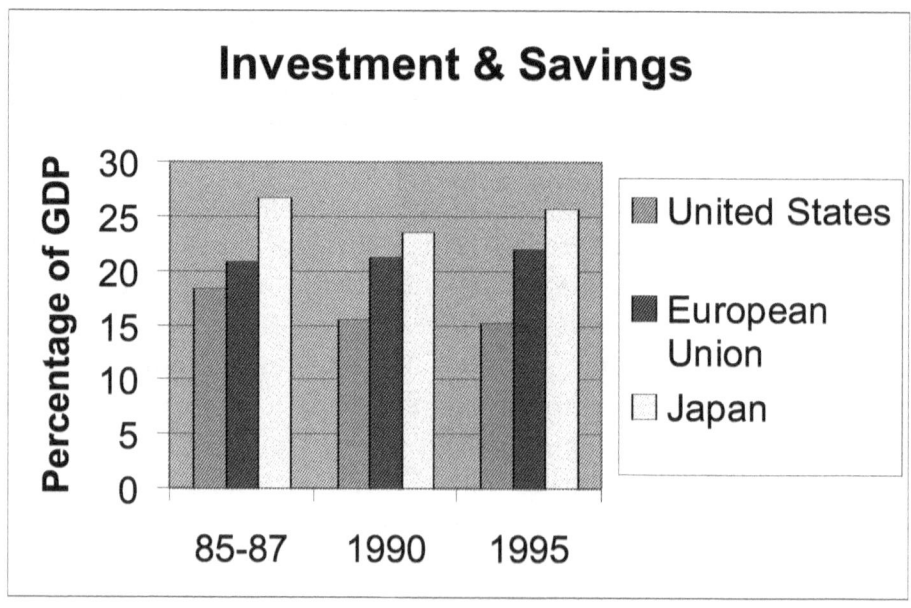

IMF

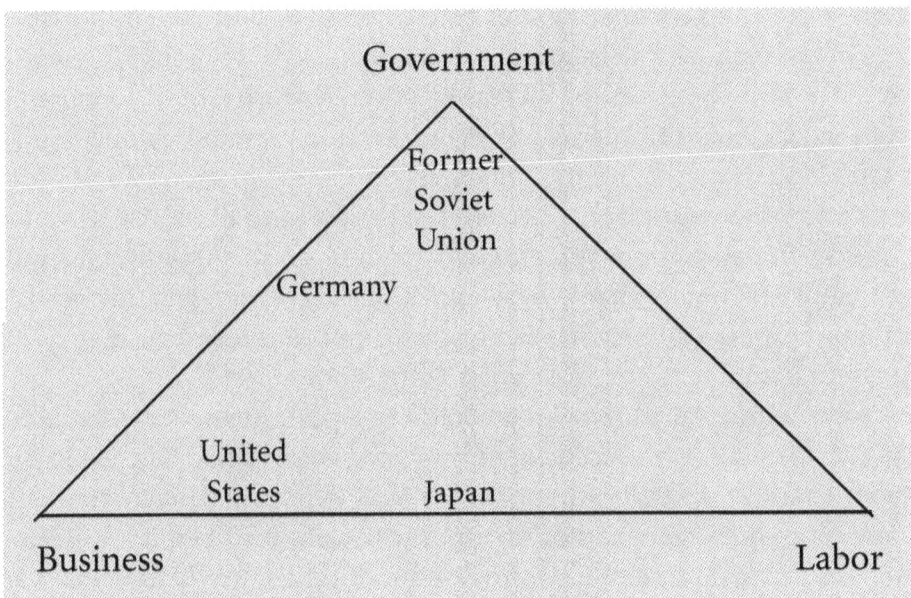

Understanding American Economic Decline, Bernstein

'The main scientific underpinning of the laissez-faire ideology is the theory that free and competitive markets bring supply and demand into equilibrium and thereby ensure the best allocation of resources. In the absence of perfect knowledge, however, both free markets and regulation are flawed. Wealth does accumulate in the hands of its owners, and if there is no mechanism for redistribution, the inequities can become intolerable.' 'The capitalist threat,' *The Atlantic Monthly*, Soros

Investment and technology go hand in hand. Both are necessary and reinforce developments in each other. Much of Asia's success can be attributed to its high savings rate combined with new opportunities in technology. For example, China saved 43% of national revenue in 1995 and significantly increased manufacturing. In comparison, sub-Sahara Africa saved only 16% in the same year and had negligible manufacturing.

National savings directly determines the amount of money available for investment. Nations use different methods to raise savings: tax policy, equity financing (bank verses stock market) and regulation among others. However, similarities can be seen in nations that have high levels of savings and, hence, investment.

After World War II the United States practiced Keynesian economics in the form of a 'mixed' economy where government, business and labor shared responsibility for investment. A lack of foreign competition allowed high consumption and short-term profitability. Until the 1970s America's 'mixed' economy produced robust productivity and an expanding middle class. When foreign manufacturers made inroads in the American market the United States needed to emphasize long-term investment rather than consumption.

However, instead of modifying the 'mixed' economy to encourage long-term investment the United States dismantled this approach and practiced laissez-faire economics. This approach cut taxes in the belief business created investment while government and labor squeezed out investment. This arrangement increased profitability but not investment. The United States has one of the lowest levels of savings of developed nations (during the late 1990s the savings rate was actually negative).

In general, Asian and European nations take a different approach. Japan uses business and labor for investment; Germany uses government and business. Germany relies on banks for equity involving long-term relationships and generous social benefits for worker training. Japanese companies extensively train workers in return for employee loyalty. Stockholders in Japan take a long-term outlook on investment. Both nations have had high levels of investment.

It appears that using more than one sector of the economy for investment leads to higher aggregate levels of investment. Wealth does accumulate within dominant sectors (whether government in the Soviet Union or business in the United States) keeping overall investment low. Just as command economies were inherently unstable due to concentration of wealth so is laissez-faire capitalism for the same reason. Nations that follow a multi-sector approach to investment seem to maximize investment.

America's 'mixed' economy came closest to producing a high investment society. A 'mixed' economy is similar to that used by Japan and Germany. However, changing back to a 'mixed' economy would require the end of laissez-faire capitalism. This would demand a change in thinking among Americans that investment outside the business sector is inefficient.

It is useful to compare America's 'mixed' economy with other successful nations that have generated high levels of investment. Both Germany and Japan have had the most successful post-World War II economies. Both have relied on using more than one sector for investment and combining cooperation with competition for economic success.

Germany has its roots of social structure from Bismarck at the turn of the 19th century. Bismarck created a rigorous social support system in order to obtain the support of workers and stymie worker discontent. Combined with this effort was an emphasis on manufacturing in order to compete with other industrialized nations. Although many Americans view the combination of strong social welfare programs with competitive industry as unworkable this system has served Germany well.

Only recently has this system come under attack by the laissez-faire system of the United States. Germany provides generous benefits to its workers. It may need to prune some of these benefits to succeed. However, this does not discredit the Rhine model of capitalism as it is sometimes called. Germany will not succeed by lowering wages to compete with America.

Only by emphasizing high-value manufacturing will Germany maintain its high wages. The key will be for Germany to balance costs and benefits in all sectors of its society.

Europe's Third Way could have been a viable contender for leading the world in the 21st century. However, because of inertia and history Asia is likely to dominate in the 21st century. Europe has a craft tradition that makes it able to make a better transition to flexible manufacturing. It also has a large middle class that has a high degree of social cohesion. Yet, Europe has many different nations with different cultures. Most importantly, Japan and other Asian nations have been able to bring the development of the microchip (the basis of the Information Revolution) in closest alignment with their cultures.

Japan is another example of a nation using several sectors of its society to compete in the world political economy. Japan's lack of natural resources and livable land are likely to have played a major role in the successful development of Japan. Japan imports nearly all of its natural resources (e.g. oil, timber and iron). Ironically, this dearth of resources is likely to have created Japan's successful social structure. Abundance of natural resources does not equate with success as classical economics might predict.

As a result of this scarcity, Japan places great emphasis on social harmony. Every sector of the economy is viewed as interrelated and potentially affecting other parts. Therefore, unlike Americans, the Japanese view nature in an interrelated way. A different sense of time is also understood where nature is understood to be more cyclical rather than linear as Americans believe.

All of these factors led Japan to structure their society for a high degree of interrelatedness. Yet, Japan is not a centrally planned economy similar to the former Soviet Union. Conversely, the Japanese have fierce competition between firms. For example, Japan's nine automobile manufacturers were already highly competitive before entering the

American marketplace. It wasn't so much competition with American firms as it was with its own that drove Japanese quality.

Japan's recent stagnation in its economy is not a sign of weakness in productivity. Japanese goods are as desired and quality-driven as ever before. The Japanese realized that the key to joining the league of wealthy nations meant having competitive high-value exports. Services were not the key to success (unfortunately, many Americans fail to realize this fact). Therefore, Japan concentrated on manufactured goods for exports while neglecting its domestic consumer markets.

To achieve this goal, Japan emphasized investment over consumption. Japan deliberately maintained high prices on consumer goods and services to ensure high employment and, hence, social harmony. Ironically, Japan has a dual economy where its manufactured exports are highly competitive while its domestic services are very inefficient.

The key will be for Japan to modernize and make competitive its domestic services without fraying its social cohesion. Ironically, the balance between consumption and investment may need to tilt toward consumption. The Japanese economy may be stuck in a situation the United States found itself in during the Great Depression when a lack of demand and surplus goods generated stagnation in the economy.

Japan has been able to transform itself in the past and there is the possibility that Japan will be able to change again. Japan should not adopt laissez-faire free markets and trade that would undermine Japan's manufacturing ability and social cohesion. Rather Japan must modernize its economy without westernizing. So far it has been successful in doing so.

China is a very large and emerging economy that is an enigma to some westerners. China has a communist political system with an increasingly capitalist economy. According to Western views, China must abandon communism and adopt Western values and social structure. Yet, the success of Japan points to a different direction. It was once said that Japan was the first successful communist country because of its emphasis on social harmony. There is no reason to believe that China will not follow a similar path and integrate its communist political system with a capitalist economy of its own making.

China has a thousand year old society. Like Japan, it derives its roots from eastern tradition and will likely modernize but not westernize. China recognizes the importance of competitive industry and actively promotes privatizing government owned industry in order to effectively compete in the world markets. Obtaining wealth is encouraged. A Chinese leader at the end of the 20th century said that 'It is glorious to get rich.'

At the same time, Chinese leaders realize the need for social cooperation and protection that competition alone cannot meet. Hence, the efforts for state intervention in different areas of society. For example, China does not allow its currency to be traded in the world markets. China, like Japan, requires that foreign companies desiring to do business in China provide critical knowledge in key industries in order to gain entry to China's markets.

Many Asian nations are following the success of Japan by combining cooperation with competition and generating investment in more than one sector of the economy. Considering the success of Japan and other Asian nations it is likely that Asia (possibly China) will provide the leading role model for successful societies in the 21st century. It is important to remember that it took Japan only several decades to challenge the supremacy of the United States. China's development will be no less spectacular. China is much bigger geographically with a billion plus population. It's influence will likely reach across the globe.

It is interesting that the two key players during the Cold War will not be likely contenders in the 21st century. Communism and capitalism were often viewed as providing opposite versions of successful societies. Yet, there are more similarities with each other than with the Asian model. Both communism and capitalism obtained their theoretical roots from the West. Both Adam Smith and Karl Marx based their ideas on the Enlightenment. Both economic systems were Western ideas emphasizing the linear progression toward an ideal state.

In an odd way, American capitalism has a structure most similar to Marxism where labor and capital are viewed as opposites and antithetical to each other. While most Europeans and Japanese view corporations as part of the social capital and workers an asset, most Americans view shareholder profitability as supreme and labor as a cost. This dichotomous approach inevitably leads to conflict between labor and capital as Karl Marx predicted. Additionally, because workers do not have a direct voice and say in business, alienation from the system is more likely just as Marx would have predicted.

As a result, not only communism (and its socialist versions) but also American laissez-faire capitalism has limited support by all but a handful of nations (mainly Anglo-Saxon nations). Outside of Great Britain and a few others not many are following the laissez-faire model of the United States. Many view American capitalism and its world institutions such as the World Bank as predatory and destructive to the well being of the world economy. The United States, rather than being the sole remaining superpower, will find itself increasingly marginalized in the world political economy with Asia leading and Europe holding its own.

3. Competition & Cooperation: Economic Democracy?

It is odd that democracy exists in the political realm but not in the economic. Democratic rights that exist outside of the workplace disappear once one enters the workplace. American labor law is based on the premise of free will meaning that both employer and employee are free to sever their work ties at anytime. However, the reality is different. Capital holds most of the cards over labor. Workers do not have the same clout as employers in most situations. Many states in the South and West have right-to-work laws reinforcing this belief. Only in a few high demand areas and the professions does worker power match that of employers.

Only recently in the United States have labor laws protecting workers been implemented. The Progressive Era under Teddy Roosevelt, New Deal under Franklin Roosevelt and Great Society under Lyndon Johnson brought some degree of protection for American workers. Health and safety laws, a minimum wage and forty hour workweek provided some measure of support for the American worker. Nonetheless, American workers have the least amount of protection of any industrial nation.

It has only been recently that companies in the United States have encouraged team workgroups, profit sharing and stock ownership. Sometimes this is after success among foreign competitors that provide a more cooperative environment. Many companies offer some form of Employee Stock Ownership Plan (ESOP). Wal-Mart is an example of one such company. Other companies have created workgroups where decision-making is done collectively. Only a few have gone so far as to have a truly employee owned firm. One example is a steel mill in the former rust belt that was sold to its employees. Yet, this falls far short of truly empowering workers.

Far more common have been massive layoffs that have created worker insecurity and the loss of union influence. Capital has more power over labor than at any time in recent history. Chainsaw Al (Al Dunlap) made a name for himself in the early 1990s by eliminating thousands of workers once he was onboard as CEO (often hired for this very reason). Other CEOs took a similar approach in order to satisfy shareholder demands for quick quarterly profit.

During the 1960s, an alternative idea of expanding democratic rights into the workplace was proposed. This idea was called economic democracy that would provide many of the same rights in the workplace as existed outside the corporation. In other words, economic democracy would match political democracy. The dichotomy in rights inside and outside the workplace would be eliminated.

Workers would own firms and hire managers rather than shareholders holding equity and managers hiring workers. Control of the workplace would truly be placed in the hands of the workers rather than distant management and shareholders. Workers would create agreed upon work rules and have the right to change them if circumstances warranted. Managers would be hired to perform direction and leadership but only so long as workers voted to keep them. A vote could be called to change leadership.

This approach is not state ownership of the means of production that Marxism promotes. Socialism, a variant of communism, promotes state ownership of large areas of the economy. For example, Great Britain nationalized several of its major industries. The extreme form was the Soviet Union that owned virtually all industry. Socialism and communism provided some measure of security and standards. However, this approach may have even further removed democracy from the workplace. Huge bureaucracies nullified worker input and, in the case of the Soviet Union, created tyranny.

The problem with capitalism is not private ownership but rather that most citizens are not owners. Although more Americans than ever own stocks only a small group own substantial amounts of stock. Half of Americans do not own any stock. Therefore, most do not hold significant power over their economic futures. Even with stock ownership control of the workplace is relegated to management. This is true in virtually all industrialized nations.

Economic democracy attempts to reconcile capitalism and communism by expanding participatory democracy into the economic realm. Capitalism divides ownership between labor and capital. Karl Marx warned about the division between the two and the inevitable conflicts that would emerge. Communism (and its socialist variants) has historically concentrated power in the hands of a few.

To a small degree nations are moving in this direction. Profit sharing plans and employee-owned firms are more common in the United States. Quality work circles and similar arrangements encourage workers to voice their opinions in the everyday operations of the firm. However, only a few American firms are truly employee controlled.

Germany has gone the furthest in promoting worker control of firms. Germany's system of co-determination gives unions half the seats on a company's supervisory boards. Labor law makes it difficult to remove workers. Furthermore, all workers receive generous benefits. Yet, these are only small steps.

Japan relies on benevolent corporate policy rather than government to provide a measure of security for workers. Major Japanese corporations still provide lifetime employment and good benefits to its workers. Quality work circles allow worker input as to the everyday operations of a plant. However, much of this arrangement is based on Japan's social cohesiveness and implicit agreement to help one another out.

Most likely, this move toward economic democracy will occur gradually with periodic outbursts for greater worker control. Ironically, laissez-faire capitalism has reduced the power of workers. It is likely that during economic downturns workers will demand a return of some of the measures of economic security previously had by workers. Already, labor in much of Europe has protested the rollback of labor protection. Workers in China and other Asian nations will demand more rights as the affluence of these nations increase.

Currently, no nation resembles a truly participatory democracy where economic democracy is a reality. It is possible that sometime in the 22nd century economic democracy will be expanded to the current equivalent of political democracy. This expansion of democracy would only be a logical conclusion to the development of democracy over the last several centuries.

IV

The Asian Century

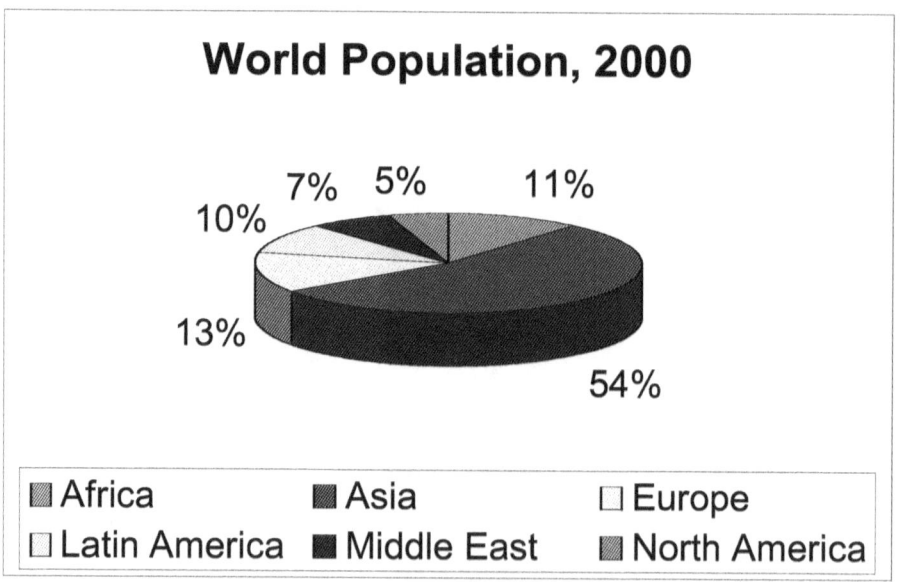

World Population, 2000

7% 5% 11%
10%
13%
54%

■ Africa   ■ Asia   □ Europe
□ Latin America   ■ Middle East   ■ North America

After World War II nations were grouped into First World (North America, Western Europe and Japan), Second World (Soviet Union and Eastern Europe) and Third World (Africa, Asia and Latin America).

The end of the Cold War with the collapse of the Soviet Union in December 1991 made this world organization obsolete.

The capitalist nations proved superior. However, the question was what form of capitalism. Successful competition from Asia and Europe undermined the American post-World War II claim to a superior and universally applicable system. Hence, three dominant forms of capitalism emerged: American, Japanese, and European.

Africa, Latin America and Middle East will remain peripheral. This is not to say that their histories are less impressive or that individual nations will not thrive. However, overall, these regions will not have the level of affluence of Asia, Europe and the United States. Many parts of Africa, with borders drawn according to European powers in the 1880s, will remain impoverished. South Africa is a bright spot. Democracy eventually will take hold in Latin America. Brazil stands as the largest nation in this region. Several oil-producing nations in the Middle East will maintain high per capita incomes. But each region as a whole will not contend for world leadership.

1. Asia: Confucian Capitalism

'Asians are destined to be world leaders in industrial, economic and trade growth in the next century. China with her mammoth population and land area will be the dominant force in the region. What happened in Japan between 1954 and 1990 is bound to happen in China, but on an imaginably greater scale.' *When Cultures Collide: Managing Successfully Across Cultures,* Lewis

The rise of Asia can be traced to Japan after World War II. The Japanese do not practice free trade or free markets. However, it is a mistake to view Japan as a centrally planned economy. The Japanese desire for harmony and reciprocity exists alongside fierce competition among companies. Corporations are viewed as social entities and invest for the long-term and train employees accordingly. Market share rather than profitability motivates business. However, Asian profitability has out-performed American corporations. Japan protects its markets using tightly organized groups of companies while limiting foreign control of its markets and firms.

Japan's long-term problem is that its form of capitalism works well within Japan but turns predatory with other nations. The Japanese are not willing to adopt free markets or free trade. An important development would be for Japan to enlarge economic reciprocity to include other nations.

After Japan's success, the Asian Tigers comprising South Korea, Taiwan, Singapore and Hong Kong followed in Japan's footsteps. Although not as wealthy as Japan, these nations are approaching or sur-passing the per capita GDP of many Western nations. Most recently, Indonesia (the world's fourth most populous nation), Malaysia, Thailand and Philippines have begun to industrialize. Other Asian nations such as Vietnam (approaching the population of Japan) will join Asia's boom.

India, with a population approaching 1 billion, will be a major player in the rise of Asia. India has a large English-speaking population, influ-ential middle-class and excellent technical institutions. Software and information technology exports will surpass 80 billion around 2003. Bangalore exemplifies a new center of technology in India.

China with its geographic size and large population will lead Asia and the world toward the middle of the 21st century. China's per capita GDP is still low ($1000 per person in 2000) but growing quickly. Together, China and India comprise one-third of the world's population.

Starting with Thailand, the Asian Crisis developed during the sum-mer of 1997 and spread to other Asian nations. Japan's economy had been stagnant after it's stock market crashed in 1989. It appears that Japan is going through a financial crisis like the United States did during the 1930s due to a lack of demand that Keynes described. Ironically, the Japanese may save too much and consume too little.

However, like the United States in the 1930s, the fundamentals of success for Japan and Asia remain. Asia has over fifty percent of the world's population and its per capita income has quadrupled after 1950, a feat never accomplished before. Asia will come to dominate the world political economy in the 21st century.

2. Europe: Social Market Capitalism

During the Cold War Europe practiced a 'Third Way' between capitalism and communism. The European temperament, even though Western, is different from America's. European's place greater emphasis on government intervention and less on market mechanisms. Importantly, many Europeans do not share American's conviction of free markets or free trade.

European nations strive to combine market economies with extensive government and labor controls. For example, European nations have national health coverage and most have 4–6 weeks vacation for all of its citizens. France has a 35-hour workweek. As a result, European nations are considerably more egalitarian with a broader middle class than the United States. Poverty and social problems are less severe.

Like Asia, corporations are viewed as social entities; shareholder profit is not the main objective. Workers and communities can often expect loyalty from companies who can, in turn, expect loyalty from them. Also, similar to Asia, profitability has outperformed American corporations.

Many Americans would be surprised to learn that Europeans have narrowed the technological gap with the United States. Europe and the United States both have strengths (Europe in wireless technology and the United States in microprocessors). Europe's productivity during the 1990s was still comparable to the United States.

The introduction of the Euro in 1999 continues the integration of Europe. Already the European Union has common citizenship for all member nations. A united E.U. will be a viable power bloc on a par with Asia and the United States.

Europe's problem is unemployment. Starting in the early 1990s, unemployment in Europe averaged ten percent, double the United State's unemployment rate. However, it does not follow that Europe should practice laissez-faire capitalism. The United States avoided higher unemployment by creating lower paid jobs. Wages and unemployment are two sides of the same coin.

Nevertheless, Europe has developed a society that many Americans remember from the 1950s and 1960s: high equality, low crime and stable institutions. The question for Europe is can it maintain its high standard of living and social equality while fostering economic growth? The 'Third Way' that many European nations desire offers a viable alternative to the laissez-faire capitalist model of the United States.

Concerning Russia, it will move toward Europe and away from its form of capitalism dominated by crime. More authoritarian Russian leaders will emerge enforcing law and order. Several former East European nations will join the European Union (e.g. Poland, Hungary and the Czech Republic) increasing Europe's influence in Russian affairs. At the same time, being a Eurasian nation, Russia will have Asian and Middle Eastern conflicts to contend with.

3. United States: Laissez-Faire Capitalism

'Future historians will not record that the 21st century belonged to the United States' 'America the Boastful,' *Foreign Affairs*, Krugman

Since the demise of the 'mixed' economy in the 1970s, the United States has practiced laissez-faire capitalism. Laissez-faire capitalism appears to generate more jobs as a result of expansion in the service sector. New business start-ups are also a strong point. America does well in creating venture capital for new enterprises.

The major weakness with laissez-faire capitalism is that it appears to sacrifice long-term investment (and profitability) for the short-term. The United States has not experienced increased productivity relative to its competitors. At the same time, inequality has greatly increased.

As mentioned, the American laissez-faire model is not likely to dominate in the 21st century. Furthermore, it will likely lag behind both Asia's Confucian capitalism and Europe's social market capitalism. The United States is likely to drift its own way with few nations other than Anglo-Saxon ones following its path.

The major issue facing the United States in the 21st century will be significant social divisions along the lines of class, gender, race, generations and community. The United States at the beginning of the 21st century already had the highest inequality among industrialized nations. These problems are not likely to diminish. Without structural change these divisions will become the defining feature of America well into the 21st century.

A. Class: High School, Vocational-Technical & College?

'Slowly and steadily we are creating a new class system, starting at birth, through early education, and finally through colleges and professional and graduate schools.' *The Next Century*, Halberstam

Class correlates with a wide variety of social experiences: country music, religious fundamentalism, weekly tabloids, Jerry Springer, monster trucks, WWF, heavy-metal and slasher movies (all closely associated with the working-class mindset). The Sex Pistols 1978 tour of the South saw this group's antagonism toward the American working class.

Social problems are predominantly concentrated among those without money. For example, there are two drug problems in America. The one of the affluent is manageable. The second of America's have-nots seems further from resolution than when the war on drugs began.

America's myth of a classless society prevents deeper understanding of class and its impact on society. Many Americans still subscribe to the idea of limitless opportunities. Failure is placed on the individual. Therefore, most support for advancement comes in the form of self-improvement.

Career Development in the United States

A.	WHAT skills do you most enjoy using? (people, ideas or information)
B.	WHERE would you most like to use those skills? (jobs, organizations and location)
C.	HOW do you identify the person who has the power to hire you? (informational interview)

1998 What Color Is Your Parachute?, Bolles

Occupation is largely the determining factor in one's socioeconomic position. Yet, the help Americans receive from social workers, guidance counselors and teachers is based on the belief that individuals control their destiny through self-awareness. Self-help books abound in resume writing, interviewing and networking. Understanding the labor market people operate within is often ignored.

Job Search Method	Effect-iveness	Jobs Most Likely Found
1. Classified ads 2. Private employment agencies 3. State employment agencies	5–20%	Low- & high-skill
4. Personal contacts 5. Direct contact	30–80%	Includes 'middle' jobs

1998 What Color Is Your Parachute?, Bolles

Labor market intermediaries (classified ads, private employment agencies and state employment agencies) do not offer much help in understanding the labor market. Jobs obtained are plentiful low-skilled jobs and hard-to-fill high-skilled jobs. Missing are the broad range of jobs that are in the middle obtained through personal or direct sources that are essentially closed to others without inside or intimate knowledge of the industry.

Occupations and Education Required in the United States

Working with People	O-J-T	Voc/Tec	College
Service	Low $		
Marketing and sales			High $
Executive, administrative and managerial			High $
Working with Information	O-J-T	Voc/Tec	College
Administrative support, including clerical	Low $		
Technicians and related support		Moderate $	
Professional specialties			High $
Working with Things	O-J-T	Voc/Tec	College
Agriculture, forestry and fishing	Low $		
Operators, fabricators, and laborers	Low $		
Precision production, craft, and repair		Moderate $	

1999 Occupational Outlook Handbook, Department of Labor

Eighty-five percent of the workforce can be covered by 250 occupations. These can be organized using Richard Bolle's Things, Information or People skills found in *What Color Is Your Parachute?* At any one time, millions of jobs are available for job-hunters in the United States. However, large differences exist in the type and pay of jobs available at any one time:

1.   **Length of Job Opening:** The average length of time a job remains open is about two weeks. Thirty-nine percent of applicants heard of a job directly from the employer, 45% heard through one additional person and only 16% heard of jobs through two or three persons. As a result, only a few people know of a job opening. Despite the large number of job openings you still have to be in the right place at the right time.

2.   **Length of Job Tenure:** Despite popular impressions, the length of employment with one employer has not changed between the 1970s and 1990s.

3.   **Lower-Paid Jobs:** Large minorities of workers move rapidly from one low paying job to another. Few people go between manual, non-manual and craft occupations. Salaries peak in the mid-thirties or early forties.

4.   **Higher-Paid Jobs:** A subset among the higher-class shows the most stable and ordered career paths. There is little movement from professions to other white-collar occupations. However, managers, sales representatives and clerks show job changes. Salaries increase into the fifties. 'Good' jobs are in protected markets or only become available at certain entry points.

5.   **Mix of Jobs:** Workers are much slower to leave good jobs. Therefore, the proportion of good jobs open at any given time is lower than their proportion in the economy.

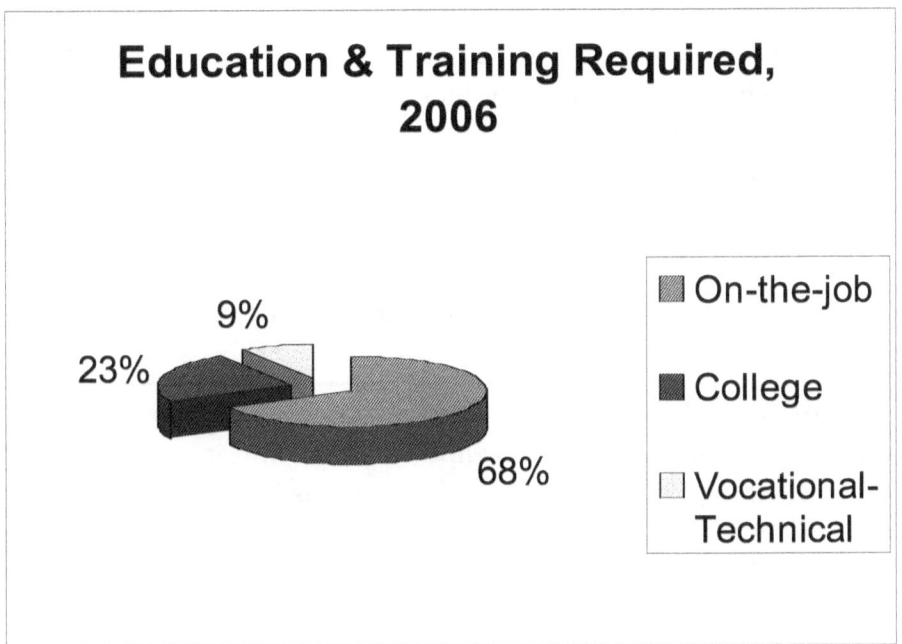

Education & Training Required, 2006

- On-the-job
- College
- Vocational-Technical

9%

23%

68%

1999 Occupational Outlook Handbook, Department of Labor

Advanced training and education is increasingly required for higher paying and desirable occupations. Americans are reminded repeatedly of the correlation (although not always causation) between the level of one's education and the expected economic earnings over one's life. As a result, educational achievement comes closest to understanding class in the United States.

Ironically, as we shall see, in the United States education has predominantly become a credential without providing employable skills. Grades are not necessarily indicative of success later in life. Many succeed later in life despite having average or sub-par grades. Those in the professions are most likely to equate intellect with success. High grades do matter in these professional occupations.

A superior system of education might be the German dual-system of learning that does away with the fiction that everyone needs a liberal arts (or high school) education. Students spend three or four days a week learning at a company, and another day and a half at a state-run vocational school. A much smaller percentage of the population attends higher education.

(1) High School: On-the-Job-Training

'This mass educational movement was prompted by the social dis-organization associated with the Industrial Revolution when primary schools were imposed on the population to instill "moral character."'
Generation On Hold, Cote & Allahar

It was not until the middle of the 19th century that the practice of formal education replaced apprenticeships as the means of acquiring work. Most did not graduate from high school until the Great Depression.

Today, a high school diploma has become the de facto degree for any job in the United States. Without this diploma even simple blue-collar jobs are likely to be out of reach. However, roughly half of the jobs available can be learned in fifteen minutes or less. As a result, there has developed significant education inflation for jobs.

A high school diploma provides predominantly social rather than academic skills. Employers desire general personality traits such as good communication, organization and teamwork. Specifics about work are taught through on-the-job training. Those who need specific skills enter vocational-training.

(2) Vocational-Technical School: Trades and Technical

Vocational-Technical Institutions and Occupational Training in the Unites States

High School (BOCES)	Secretarial, cosmetology, auto repair, nurse aide care and electronics
Technical Institute	Computer technology and programming, automotive repair and medical equipment
Trade Apprenticeship	Construction trades (carpenter, plumber and electrician), laboratory technicians and horse trainer
Armed Forces	Precision production and craft and repair

'Job training: Who needs it and where to get it,' *Occupational Outlook Quarterly,* Amirault

Some of the fastest growing occupational segments require some training beyond high school but no college. Unfortunately, in the United States, vocational-technical training is fragmented and without formal organization. Unlike nations like Germany with a formal training and apprenticeship system, most Americans rely on high school preparation (e.g. BOCES) and a variety of for-profit vocational schools. The Armed Forces have proven to be good training for many occupations.

Canada provides a system of colleges that complements its degree granting university system. Canadian colleges offer diploma, certificate and apprenticeship/training programs in a wide array of occupations. Up to thirty percent of college students already have a university degree. Canada's system of colleges is much more organized than in the United States.

(3) College? Professional and Managerial

> 'By the 1880s, educational entrepreneurs finally realized that many people considered the classical education they offered irrelevant. To make campus life fun, the scholarly model gave way to the socializing model.' *Generation On Hold,* Cote & Allahar

Until the middle of the 20th century college was an elite experience for the upper class to socialize their children for leadership roles in American society. After World War II, higher education significantly expanded so that college has become a rite of passage and de facto requirement for the middle class (much as it had for the upper-class in the late 19th century). Increasingly, education is becoming K-16 (or at least K-14) for middle class Americans. However, caveat emptor before considering the benefits of college.

First, *fifty percent of occupational attainment is attributable to family background.* The choice of college has only a minor influence on occupational achievement when considering student characteristics upon entering college. More successful individuals are likely to attend college resulting in a self-fulfilling prophecy that college creates success.

Second, *socialization with like-minded aspiring professionals through fraternities and sororities, sports and campus life are the most important benefits of college.* Employers cite communication skills as more important than coursework, major and GPA in hiring. Outside of the professions, having high grades does not necessarily enhance employment opportunities.

Third, *upon graduation, alumni contacts play an important role in obtaining work.* College is a version of the old boys' network where the success of alumni helps determine the success of graduates.

College Graduate Underemployment

1967	1970	1975	1980	1985	1990
11.7%	11.3%	16.7%	18.6%	19.2%	19.9%

'Are more college graduates really taking 'high school' jobs,' *Monthly Labor Review,* Tyler et al.

Percent of Population Attending College

Germany	11.6%
Great Britain	10.7%
France	10.2%
United States	23.6%

'The tyranny of the diploma,' *Forbes,* McMenamin

During the latter part of the 20th century the value of higher education in the United States has eroded (similar to the eroding value of high school earlier). In 1970, only one in seven workers (14%) had a college degree compared with one in four workers (25%) in 1990. As a result, jobs that previously required only a high school degree now required college. Whereas once a college degree brought elite pay, it now only brings middle class pay. Interestingly, the largest employer of college graduates during the 1990s was Enterprise-Rent-A-Car who preferred fraternity or sorority experience. In general, college degrees have become a commodity:

1. **On-campus Recruitment:** 5% of college graduates are placed through on-campus interviews.

2. **Time to Obtain Work:** 9–12 months is the average length of time graduates take to find an entry-level job.

3. **Entry-level Pay:** A significant portion of graduates start near the minimum wage.

4.   **Entry-level Job Retention:** 75% of college graduates quit their first job.

5.   **Type of Employer:** The traditional goal of working for Fortune 500 companies is unlikely unless one holds a professional or technical degree (large corporation provide significantly less employment than at the peak in the early 1970s). Furthermore, employment results in only one or two advancements for most.

6.   **Type of Occupation:** Retail, insurance and banking are major industries where college graduates are hired in large numbers. Many graduates resort to jobs in lower-level management, sales and clerical.

7.   **Average Lifetime Salary:** Typical salary levels are similar to those earned by teachers. Twenty-one percent of college graduates earn less than the average for a high school graduate. Top college earners in management, sales, law and medicine distort average college earnings.

Importance of Institution

Higher Education in the United States

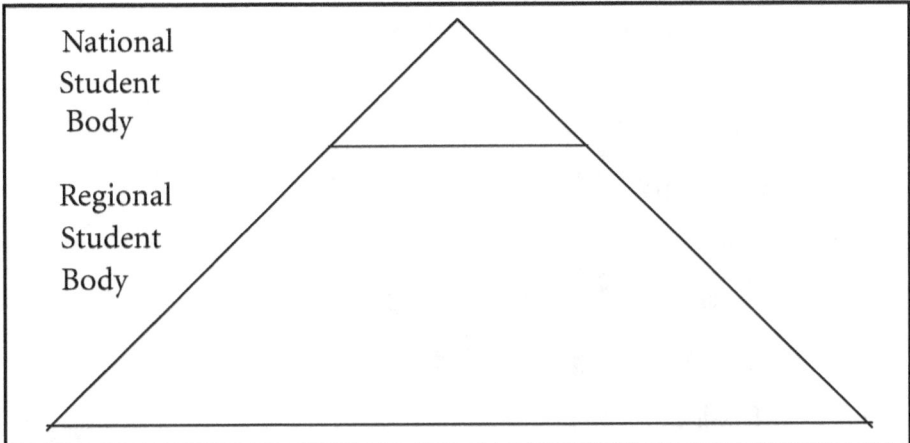

National universities and colleges (those with a national and increasingly international student body) confer more value to a graduate's degree. The majority of students attend regional public universities and colleges that have been upgraded from teacher colleges. There has been a vocationalization of the liberal arts at these schools where students with generally lower socioeconomic background demand job skills.

Importance of Major

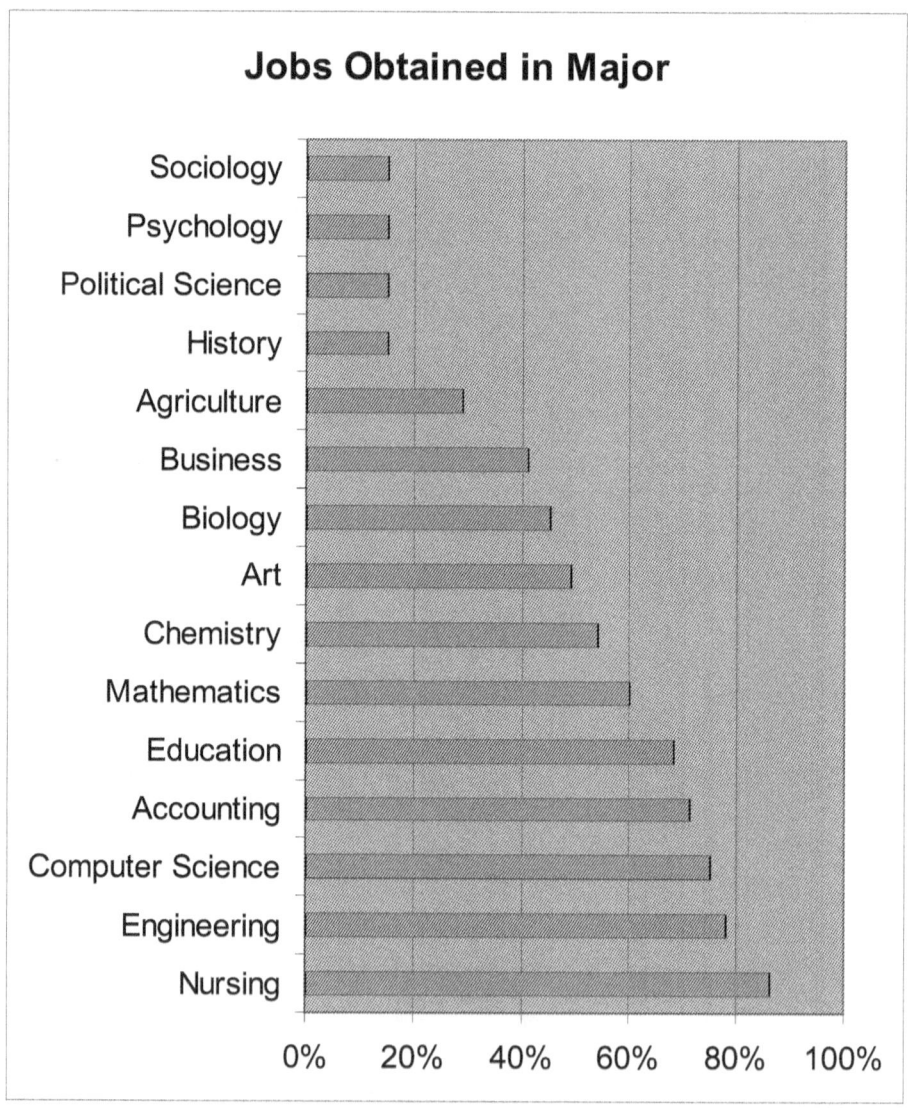

The Right Place at the Right Time, Wegmann & Chapman

In general, majors required by professions have the highest proportion of graduates employed in the graduate's major. Many large companies will only interview professional or technical graduates. Liberal arts degrees and vocationally oriented degrees not required by a profession will not likely provide job skills.

(A) Professional Degrees with Job-Skills: Professions

'There are two ways to interpret the better performance of professionals relative to other workers in the new, internationalized economy. The most common explanation (the one preferred by the overclass and its publicists in the major new media) is that the world economy, in some vague way, rewards expertise and high-tech skills.

A more plausible explanation is that professionals in the United States benefit from a vigorously enforced form of protectionism based on credentials and licensing.' 'To have and have not,' *Harpur's*, Lind

Although a well-rounded liberal arts graduate is cited as an asset, most graduates hired for their major have obtained professional training in a specific field. Oftentimes, state licensing and certification require the successful completion of specific coursework. In these cases, coursework, major and grade point average (GPA) are central to getting hired. Increasingly, requirements for professions have lengthened to five years of study.

PROFESSIONAL MAJOR	JOB PROSPECTS
Accounting	Accounting companies looking for management accountants and CPAs require the bachelor's degree in accounting
Architecture	Most states require a bachelor's degree in architecture to qualify for the licensing exam.
Nursing	Nursing requires college coursework in nursing to become a registered nurse.
Engineering	Engineering licensing in most states requires a bachelor's in engineering.
Teaching	To teach in public schools a bachelor's in education is most often required.

The Career Atlas, Kuenstler; Landing Your First Real Job, Linn

(B) Liberal Arts Degrees without Job-Skills: Sales/Customer Service

'To be sure, people with liberal arts degrees occasionally find business-related career opportunities outside the fields of sales and marketing. But this is actually very rare.' *Shy-Man Syndrome,* Gilmartin

In general, national universities and colleges have maintained a traditional liberal arts curriculum: humanities, social sciences and science. These top-ranked national universities and colleges typically do not offer job related majors. It is assumed (often correctly) that specific job skills can be learned on the job.

Many regional colleges and universities offer job related liberal arts majors (for example, management and marketing). Unless a college offers a particularly strong program, these majors do not provide job skills. Liberal arts degrees in marketing, mass communication and management, among others, are designed to attract enrollment. These degrees provide specialized skills not useful until one gains job experience if at all.

Liberal arts graduates are most likely hired for the ability to communicate and interact with others. Although the broad liberal arts experience is cited as the greatest strength of these graduates the social skills learned outside the classroom are most important. *Seventy percent of liberal arts graduates find work related to sales (e.g. insurance, retail and banking).*

LIBERAL ARTS MAJOR	JOB PROSPECTS
Advertising	According to the AAAA, this degree is not valued by agencies. Obtaining work requires working in a job below the one desired.
Public Relations	Your appearance, personal contacts and portfolio are the ways to get hired. Again, internships are crucial.
Radio, television and performing arts	Credentials do not carry much weight in obtaining employment with the exception of technical production skills. Talent, image and creativity count for most.
Journalism	Only one-fifth of graduates take jobs at newspapers and magazines. In addition, the profession has no uniform opinion about appropriate training ('The slow, sad sellout of journalism school, *Rolling Stone*, October 16, 1997).
Business/ Management	In the past, management-in-training programs hired graduates. Today, this is much less true. Management is not an entry-level position; it must be obtained indirectly. At most, business schools can be expected to teach about business, not how to do it.
Human Resource Management	One needs experience in one's industry. Starting out in sales or as a secretary is common.
Marketing	Working in sales is the entry-level route to advancement to marketing.
Environmental Science	Interdisciplinary degrees in the environment (e.g. wildlife management, forestry, etc.) do not offer the depth of knowledge required to enter these fields.

The Career Atlas, Kuenstler; *Landing Your First Real Job,* Linn

Importance of Experience: Cooperatives/Internships

College degrees are necessary, but not sufficient for most college-level positions. Previously, college graduates could count on large corporations providing training. However, this is much less true today. Corporations will not spend money on expensive training programs when other means are available. Specifically, college graduates are increasingly expected to obtain experience before graduating. For example, a leader in experiential learning has been Antioch University. *Seventy percent of graduates have experience in a cooperative program, internship or externship.*

1. Cooperative Program	Cooperative programs are part of your college major.
2. Internship	Internships involve work experience related to one's major.
3. Externship	Externships are brief work experiences (a few weeks).

Graduate School?

'If you do not know why you are getting the degree, you probably should not get one. You can sort out career options just as easily while being paid to work as you can while paying tuition. To be blunt: Going to graduate or professional school because you do not know what else to do is foolish.' 'Is there another degree in your future? Choosing among professional and graduate schools,' *Occupational Outlook Quarterly*, Baxter

An increasing number of bachelor degree graduates decide on obtaining a graduate degree. However, the greater number of individuals pursuing advanced degrees has created education inflation much as it has for undergraduate degrees. Whereas once a bachelor's degree was sufficient for advancement now a master's is often required. Therefore, the problems graduates face are similar to those of undergraduates:

1. **Importance of Institution:** Quality is uneven among programs. For example, only graduates from the top ranked MBA programs obtain commensurate job prospects. For graduates among the other 800 MBA programs in the United States, the MBA is a way of limiting the applicant pool rather than providing job skills.

2. **Importance of Major:** Again, degrees required by professions (e.g. law and medicine) provide job skills. Other majors generally do not. For example, MBA graduates enter relatively few fields involving economic analysis: investment banking or consulting (85%).

3. **Importance of Experience:** Many employers desire experience rather than an advanced degree. For example, Harvard's MBA program requires two years or more of job experience before considering applicants.

Even at the Ph.D. level, employment prospects are mixed. During the 1990s Ph.D. employment in the humanities was particularly dismal (29% underemployment). However, even in the higher demand areas of engineering and science, Ph.D. graduates are having difficulty finding work (12-25% underemployment). In some fields, postdoctoral work is increasingly required.

Sources of Employment Statistics

Many media sources use the National Association of Colleges and Employer's Salary Survey published in January for college graduate employment statistics. It is important to remember that these results are averages. The *U.S. News & World Report's Annual Guide to Colleges* is the most widely available resource for understanding college rankings. Additionally, *The Occupational Outlook Quarterly* and Bureau of Labor Statistic's *Monthly Labor Review* provides periodic information on college graduate employment. *The Gorman Report* ranks the quality of majors at different schools both at the undergraduate and graduate level.

B. Gender: Male & Female

'Instead of bad choices inducing teen pregnancy that then causes lower adult earnings, it may be that realistic expectations of lower adult earnings induce some women to bear children relatively early, because the economic opportunity costs of doing so are likely to be fairly low in the first place.

One of the principal causes of the "breakup" of the traditional family, in short, would appear to be the relative decline in male earnings. Men have had less and less to offer women economically to keep them in bad marriages.' *Fat and Mean*, Gorden

Single Parent Families

	Under $14,763	$25,000–100,000	Above $100,000
Single Mother	52%	8%	3%
Single Father	6%	3%	2%

Annual Report of the United States, 1996; Bagby

A major news story in 1996 concerned a poor African-American male, Nushawn Williams, discovered passing AIDS through unprotected sex to poor teenage girls. The story of Nushawn Williams alluded to the interaction between gender, race and class and highlighted the lack of incentives for delaying pregnancy or staying married among poor Americans.

While many affluent women benefited from increased opportunities in the professions, blue-collar women have seen reduced opportunities in higher-pay manufacturing jobs. The reduced gap in earnings between men and women is due mainly to male wages falling rather than female wages rising. Furthermore, occupations at the bottom of the socioeconomic ladder are still predominantly gender segregated.

Changing economic fortunes may have contributed to the gender gap started with Ronald Reagan's election in 1980. Men have predominantly voted Republican while women tended to vote Democratic (Bob Dole would have won the 1996 presidential election if only men had voted).

Increased inequality will only intensify gender differences as women and men compete for fewer partners able to earn a living wage. As a result, it is likely that crimes of sexual violence (rape, incest, etc) will remain high in the United States.

1.	Average number of sexual partners over last year: 0 or 1 (83%).
2.	Most Americans date those of similar age, race, education and religion.
3.	School and work (locations where one is at for a period of time) are the most likely places to meet partners.

Sex in America, Michael, et al.

Economics will likely overshadow the sexual revolution of the 1960s. The zipless fuck advocated in *The Fear of Flying* (1973) failed to deliver while AIDS tainted the guilt-free attitude of the *Joy of Sex* (1975). The sexual revolution produced selective changes. For example, teenagers practice safe sex and over half of adults live together before marrying while some recommend pursuing more than one person at a time to generate confidence.

Baby boomers are not of the hedonistic mindset when raising their children. For the first time in 20 years, the percentage of sexually active high school students decreased (54% in 1991, 48% in 1997). Sexual behavior will likely become more conservative over the next twenty years as boomers raise their children. Americans remain puritanical in their attitudes toward sexuality (for example, read 'Americans retain puritan attitudes on matters of sex,' *The Wall Street Journal*, March 5, 1998).

Worldwide, the return of the Great Mother figure attests to some success in gender equality. Urbanization had given rise to the withdrawal of women from the workforce and placed men at the center of power in villages; war replaced the hunting group. Nonetheless, the degree of gender equality varies greatly across the world. In general, less developed regions (e.g. Africa, Latin America and Middle East) experience greater gender inequality.

The remaining major issue for the women's movement is the conflict between work and child rearing for women. Most industrial nations provide generous maternity leave benefits with the important exception of the United States. The lack of comprehensive national health care and lack of maternal benefits leaves many single women in poverty in the United States.

The next gender revolution may deal with men demanding a more equitable role in society. Men disproportionately take the most dangerous jobs from heavy work to warfare. While the women's movement has expanded possibilities for women, the social realm for men has diminished in important respects. Respect for physical labor in manufacturing is of decreasing importance while outlets for constructive expression for men is still limited. It is possible that during the next spiritual awakening around the 2040's men will start a new gender revolution.

C. Race and Ethnicity: Black & White (& increasingly Brown)

'We believe that it is not so much race discrimination that is the problem, though that continues to be serious enough, but, rather, the racialization of the class hierarchy-the Brazilianization of America, as Michael Lind calls it. Class differences transcend race and divide all Americans.' *Habits of the Heart*, Bellah

Julius O. Wilson wrote in *The Declining Significance of Race* that race had become less important than class. His statement seems validated by the rise of affluent African-Americans while poor African-Americans have been hurt particularly hard by the loss of higher paid manufacturing jobs.

However, the O.J. Simpson trail highlighted America's continuing problems with race. Whites and blacks viewed the fairness of the outcome very differently. African-Americans generally supported the verdict while whites did not. America still has a long way to go to resolving the race problem.

The most important development in the 21st century concerning race and ethnicity will be the increasing importance of the Hispanic population. In 2005, Hispanics will be the largest minority surpassing African-Americans. In 2050, 25% of the United States will likely speak Spanish as their primary language. African-American and Hispanic competition for similar resources will likely be a new source of conflict.

D. Generations: Puritanism & Hedonism

Idealists	Idealists usher in a period of **spiritual awakening (inner-driven era)** leaving institutions to decay.
Reactives	Reactives attempt to slow the pace of change of spiritual awakening.
Civics	Civics attempt **civic renewal (outer-driven era)** while neglecting the spiritual.
Adaptives	Adaptives conform to civic renewal and later embrace spiritual awakening as cycle repeats.

The Fourth Turning, Strauss & Howe

During the 1992 presidential election Vice President Dan Quayle criticized television's popular fictional character Murphy Brown when she decided to have a child without a father calling it simply another lifestyle choice. Quayle received considerable derision and was thought as being out of touch with reality. Surprisingly, just a few years later Quayle's view no longer generated outcry. In fact, President Bill Clinton routinely emphasized the importance of two-parent families.

This example illuminates the cyclical nature of American history when a new generation comes of age. American history oscillates between inner spiritual awakenings and outer civic renewals. Much of the change involves America's conflict with Puritanism and hedonism. The United States has had four periods of spiritual awakenings: the Great Awakening (1730s–1760s), the Second Great Awakening (1800s–1830s), the Third Great Awakening (1870s–1900s) and 1960s–2000s. Each led to a major upheaval in American history: American Revolution, Civil War, World War II and the next upheaval in the first decades of the 21st century.

The baby boom generation ushered in the most recent spiritual awakening. The large number of idealist baby boomers has intensified their generational narcissism. As the nation moves toward the next civic crisis in the first decades of the 21st century boomers will become increasingly more judgmental. 'Zero tolerance' is one example where boomers have reinstated the values they once rebelled against. The children of boomers, the Millennium generation, will be given the job to rebuild American civic life. If they fail it is unlikely that any generation will succeed in the 21st century.

E. Community: Town & Country

> 'As Columbia University historian Kenneth T. Jackson says "The United States is not only the world's first suburban nation, but it will also be the last. The earth cannot sustain any more economies like ours."' *Save Our Land, Save Our Towns*, Hylton & Seitz

In developed nations affluent central business districts with impoverished neighborhoods are surrounded by increasingly wealthier neighborhoods as one moves further from urban centers. Developing nations have this pattern reversed; cities developed before industrialization. Therefore, urban areas are affluent while outlying industrial areas are poor. For example, Latin American cities exhibit this pattern.

The United States stands alone in the extent of urban sprawl and neighborhood segregation. More than 80,000 municipalities fragments and divides metropolitan planning. Only the United States has experienced large growth in its exurbs. Tyson Corners, a gas station corner after World War II, has developed into a major metropolitan area rivaling downtown Washington, D.C. for development.

Tucson, Arizona is an example of American community planning in the extreme: spread out development with little core city and large wealth differences between neighborhoods. Contrast this with Toronto,

Ontario where thirty percent of all new housing in every municipality is required to be affordable to low- and moderate-income residents. Regional government spreads the burden of taxation and services. The result is less urban sprawl and income polarization.

It is questionable whether American communities offer a viable model for other nations. America's vast continental distance may allow for this type of development. But it does not seem economically efficient or equitable for other nations with fewer resources and space. Sprawl depletes the tax base and requires excessive maintenance of sewer lines, roads and infrastructure (compact development costs only a third to half as much).

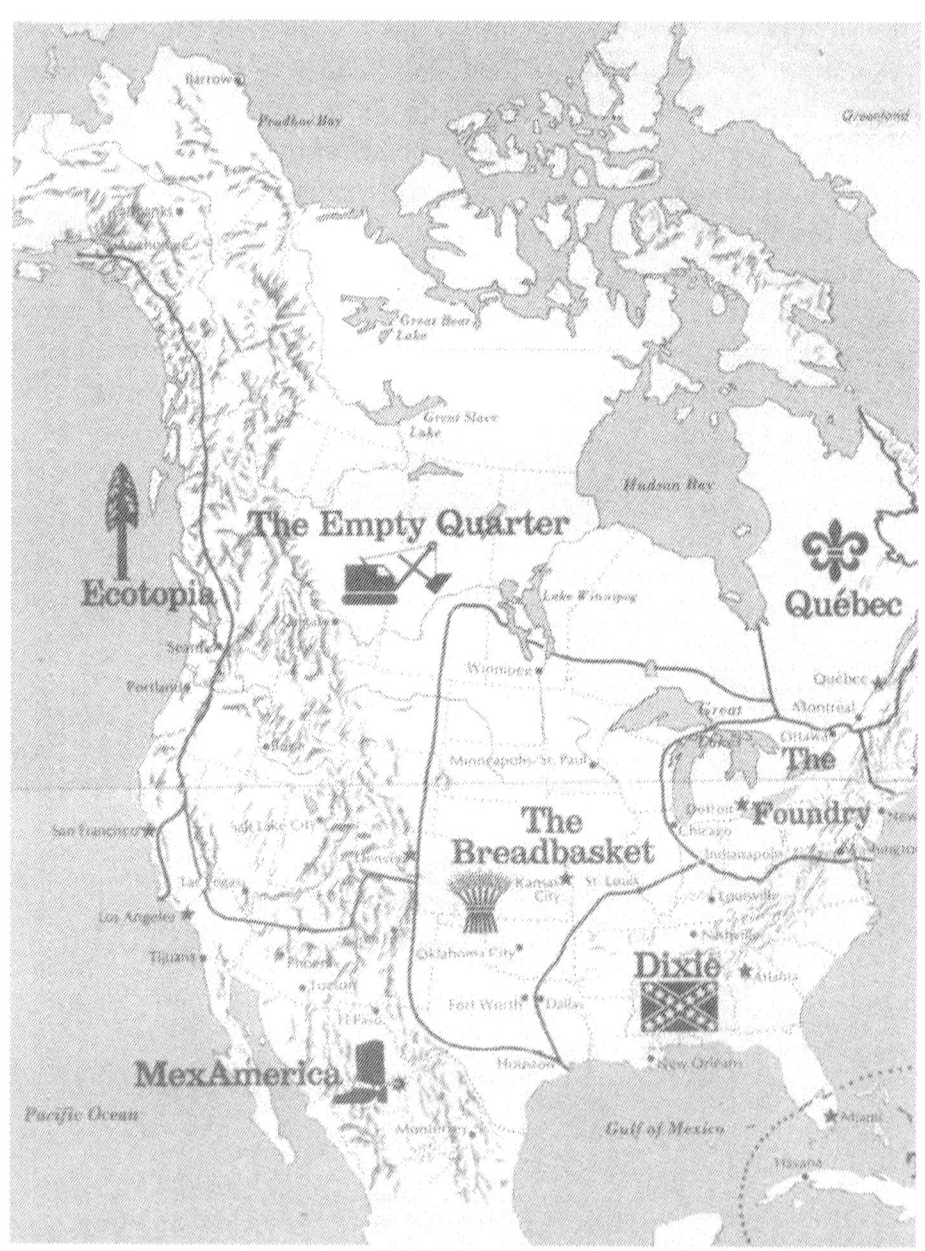

The Nine Nations of North America, Gaffeau

The Nine Nations of North America outlines nine regions with different social, political and economic characteristics. Each region is distinct as a result of geography and history intersecting.

The rise of the South has been a success story at the end of the 20th century. The poverty and racial segregation of the South made it virtually a different country as recently as 1940. Since, the South experienced significant growth. The South, along with the West, will gain population and political representation into the 21st century.

At the same time, the industrial Northeast and Midwest declined. The Northeast no longer controlled events through the eastern liberal establishment. Instead, these regions became more like the South while the South became more like the Northeast and Midwest. Power has spread throughout regions (California, Texas, New York, and Florida are the four most populous states).

> 'As unbelievable as it may be to late-20th century citizens of the U.S., emigration may be a more common trend in the next century.' 'Escape from America,' *Money*, Belsky

Money magazine did a five-month investigation that suggests record numbers of Americans are moving abroad for better lives. Even more important, those most likely to leave are the best educated and wealthiest. Some Americans believe that the nation they are living in is not the one they grew up in. "There is a sense that things have gone too far in the wrong direction," says one interviewee.

America Compared with Our Northern Neighbor: Canada

> 'Throughout the period between 1961 and 1995, Canada's performance was superior to America's in all respects except the rate of unemployment. The quiet depression of the 1990s has been louder north of the border because of high joblessness.' *The Great American Deception*, Batra

Significant Differences	Canada	United States
Most important national issue	Jobs	World Affairs
Most important objective	Economy	Family
Poverty	7%	13%
Violent crime per 100,000 (1996)	269	598
Unemployment rate (1993)	11.2%	6.8%
Abortion rate per 1,000	175	401
Birth to teenagers	6%	13%
Welcome more sexual freedom	40%	29%
Health-care expenditures (GDP%)	9%	12%
Believe in hell	34%	60%
Marriages ending in divorce	28%	43%
Gun ownership	3%	24%
View other country as different	43%	21%

Borderlines, Sauve; 'How different we are,' *Maclean's*, Corelli; 'A survey of Canada,' *The Economist*

Many Americans fail to understand how government and institutions make a difference in a nation's well being. Whereas Americans fought the

American Revolution, Canadians did not. This has encouraged Americans to distrust government and Canadians to view it as a public good more like Europeans.

Canadians have a stronger commitment to equality and justice and are more law-abiding. National health care and a stronger social welfare system have helped Canada avoid the severity of social problems that plague the United States. Additionally, less financialization has occurred in its economy. The Toronto Stock Exchange, created in 1987, doubled through 2000 while the Dow Jones Industrial Average increased 350%.

Unlike Americans, who overwhelmingly regard themselves as conservative, fifty-six percent of Canadians call themselves liberals and have a commitment to liberal social values. Extremes in politics and religion are noticeably muted with the exception of Quebec's desire for a distinct society.

> 'We have noted over the past two years that Canadians were prepared to accept (with resignation if not enthusiasm) a future of diminished opportunities. We have never, however, been able to detect a population that was willing to turn its back on a tradition of civility, tolerance and concern for the welfare of those less well-off than themselves. That has been-and appears likely to continue to be-the single greatest hallmark of our self-identification as Canadians. 'A confident nation,' *Maclean's*, Gregg

Canadians voted out of power all but a handful of the ruling Progressive Conservative Party during 1993. Canada, like the United States, witnessed loss of faith in its institutions and national leaders as Canadian incomes stagnated and manufacturing jobs disappeared.

However, unlike the United States, Canadians kept their commitment to equality. Canadian inequality did not increase during the 1980s and 1990s as it did in the United States. Furthermore, even in productivity, Canada seems to be pulling ahead according to an OECD report. Even though Canada may decline relative to other industrial nations, it is likely that Canada will have a higher standard of living than the United States.

About the Author

I did not start out with the intention of writing a book. Rather, the book largely evolved out of my work experiences. In retrospect, many of these jobs exposed me to facets of America not normally seen. Understanding my work history is a good way to understand my perspective in writing *Wealth in the 21st Century*.

Work History

5/00–	Owner (graphic design)	Home-Mart (Vestal, NY)
8/98–	Sales Representative & Photographer	Vantine Studios (Hamilton, NY)
6/99–8/99	Carton Sorter	Frito-Lay (Kirkwood, NY)
12/98–1/99	Assembler	Amphenol (Endwell, NY)
6/98–8/98	Assembler	Lander (Binghamton, NY)
6/2/98	General Laborer	Greenblott Metal (Binghamton, NY)
1/94–5/98	Photographer & Marketing Consultant	Fraternal Composite Service (Utica, NY)

1/98	Scope Inspector	Dovatron International (Binghamton, NY)
11/97 & 1/98	Floorshow Associate	Peter Trapp Computer Shows (Binghamton, NY)
9/97–10/97	Merchandiser	National Retail Services (Binghamton, NY)
8/97–9/97	Shipper/Receiver	Shapiro's (Endicott, NY)
7/97 & 9/97	Courtesy Caller	Time-Warner Cable (Vestal, NY)
6/97	Packer	Matthew Bender (Conklin, NY)
5/97–6/97	Merchandiser	PIA (Binghamton, NY)
9/96–5/97	Owner (discount products)	Home-Mart (Vestal, NY)
12/94–1/95	Ski Lift Operator	Mount Tone Ski Resort (Lake Como, PA)
94 Summer	Photographer	Lauren Studios (Vestal, NY)
12/93–1/94	Driver	Pizza Hut (Endwell, NY)
8/93–11/93	Photographer	Varden Studios (Rochester, NY)
10/90–8/93	Driver	Domino's Pizza (Binghamton, NY)
10/90	Solderer	SCI (Owego, NY)

90 Summer	Counselor	YMHA/YWHA Cedar Lake Camp (Milford, PA)
2/90–5/90	Driver	Subway (Vestal, NY)
2/90–6/93	Teacher, Substitute	Chenango Valley Schools (Binghamton, NY) Owego-Apalachin Central Schools (Owego, NY)
12/89–1/90	Inventory Handler	Barnes & Noble (Binghamton, NY)
88 & 89 Summer	Administrative Assistant	Camp Wayne-Girls (Preston Park, PA)
4/88	Fast Food Worker	Arby's (Johnson City, NY)
11/87–4/88	Bookseller	Coles Bookstore (Johnson City, NY)
87 Summer	Laminator	IBM (Endicott, NY)
86 Summer	Conference Assistant	Conference Office, Binghamton University (Binghamton,NY)
9/79–5/85	Paperboy	Press & Sun-Bulletin (Binghamton, NY)

Education

January 2001	Wildlife/Forestry Conservation Career Diploma	Harcourt Learning Direct (Scranton, PA)
June 2000	Small Business Start-Up Certificate	Broome Community College (Binghamton, NY)
December 1989	M.A. Liberal Arts	SUNY-Plattsburgh (Plattsburgh, NY)
May 1988	B.S. Management	Binghamton University (Binghamton, NY)
June 1983	New York State Regents	Vestal High School (Vestal, NY)

Bibliography

I. The American Century

Albert, Michel. *Capitalism Vs. Capitalism.* New York: Four Wall Eight Windows, 1993.

Bluestone, Barry & Harrison, Bennett. *The Deindustrialization of America.* New York: Basic Books, 1982.

Gottlieb, Annie. *Do You Believe in Magic?* New York: Times Books, 1987.

Hacker, Andrew. *The End of the American Era.* New York: Antheneum, 1970.

Halberstam, David. *The Next Century.* New York: Morrow, 1991.

Hodgson, Robert S. *America In Our Time.* Garden City: Doubleday, 1978.

Kennedy, Paul. *Preparing for the 21st Century.* New York: Random House, 1993.

Lyons, Paul. *Class of '66.* Philadelphia: Temple University Press, 1994.

Madrick, Jeffrey. *The End of Affluence.* New York: Random House, 1995.

McElvaine, Robert S. *What's Left?* Holbrook, Massachusetts: Adams Media Corp., 1996.

New York Times Staff. *The Downsizing of America.* New York: Times Books, 1996.

Phillips, Kevin. *Arrogant Capital*. Boston: Little, Brown and Co., 1994. *The Emerging Republican Majority*. New Rochelle, NY: Arlington House, 1969.

Putnam, Robert D. *Bowling Alone*. New York: Simon & Schuster, 2000.

Whitman, David. *The Optimism Gap: The I'm Ok—They're Not Syndrome and the Myth of American Decline*. New York: Walker and Co., 1998.

II. Measuring Wealth: Efficiency and Equality

Braun, Dennis D. *The Rich Get Richer*. Chicago: Nelson-Hall, 1997.

Galbraith, James K. *Created Unequal: The Crisis in American Pay*. New York: Free Press, 1998.

Hacker, Andrew. *Money*. New York: Scribner, 1997.

Krugman, Paul. *The Age of Diminished Expectations*. Cambridge: MIT Press, 1994.

'Mapping income inequality.' *USA Today* 20 September 1996: 3B.

Overberg, Paul. 'Digging for roots of income inequality.' *USA Today* 23 September 1996: 2B.

Peters, Werner. *Society On the Run: A European View of America*. Armonk, NY: M.E. Sharpe, 1996.

Porter, Michael E. *The Competitive Advantage of Nations*. New York: Free Press, 1990. *On Competition*. Boston: Harvard Business School, 1996.

Wolff, Michael. *Where We Stand*. New York: Bantam Books, 1992.

III. Creating Wealth: Cooperative Investment and Competitive Manufacturing

Attali, Jacques. *Millennium*. New York: Times Books, 1991.

Barlett, Donald L. & Steele, James B. *America: Who Stole the Dream?* Kansas City: Andrews and McMeel, 1996.

Batra, Ravi. *The Great American Deception*. New York: John Wiley and Sons, 1996.

Bernstein, Michael A. & Adler, David E. *Understanding American Economic Decline*. Cambridge: Cambridge University Press, 1994.

Dertouzos, Michael, et al. *Made in America*. Cambridge, Mass.: MIT Press, 1989.

Fingleton, Eamonn. *In Praise of Hard Industries*. Boston: Houghton Mifflin, 1999.

Gorden, David M. *Fat and Mean*. New York: Martin Kessler Books, 1996.

Jonas, Norman. 'The hollow corporation.' *Business Week* 3 March 1986: 56.

'The reindustrialization of America.' *Business Week* 30 June 1980: 55.

IV. The Asian Century

Amirault, Thomas. 'Job training: who needs it and where they get it.' *Occupational Outlook Quarterly* Winter 1992–93: 18.

Astin, Alexander. *What Matters in College*. San Francisco: Jossey-Bass, 1993.

Baxter, Neale. 'Is there another degree in your future? Choosing among professional and graduate schools.' *Occupational Outlook Quarterly* Winter 1993–94: 18.

Bagby, Meredith E. *Annual Report of the United States, 1996.* New York: Harper Business, 1996.

Bellah, et al. *Habits of the Heart.* Berkeley: University of California Press, 1996.

Belsky, Gary. 'Escape from America.' *Money* July 1994: 60.

Bolles, Richard Nelson. *The 1998 What Color Is Your Parachute?* Berkeley: Ten Speed Press, 1997.

Corelli, Rae. 'How different we are.' *Maclean's* 4 November 1996: 36.

Cote, James E. & Allahar, Anton L. *Generation On Hold.* New York: New York University Press, 1994.

Employment Outlook: 1994–2005. United States Labor Department, 1995.

Farrell, Warren. *Why Men Are The Way They Are.* New York: McGraw-Hill, 1986.

Garreau, Joel. *The Nine Nations of North America.* Boston: Houghton Mifflin, 1981.

Gilmartin, Brian G. *The Shy-Man Syndrome.* Landam, MD: Madison Books, 1989.

Gray, John. *False Dawn.* New York: The New Press, 1998.

Gregg, Allen. 'A confident nation: a new poll shows growing optimism.' *Maclean's* 29 December 1997: 16.

Greider, William. *One World, Ready or Not.* New York: Simon & Schuster, 1997.

Hylton, Thomas & Seitz, Blair. *Save Our Land, Save Our Towns.* Harrisburg, PA: RB Books, 1995.

'Just how productive is Canada?' *Maclean's* 5 April 1999: 48.

Kerbo, Harold. *Social Stratification and Inequality.* Boston: McGraw-Hill, 2000.

Kuenstler, Gail. *The Career Atlas.* Franklin Lakes, NJ: Career Press, 1996.

Krugman, Paul. 'America the boastful.' *Foreign Affairs* May 1998: 32.

Lewis, Richard D. *When Cultures Collide: Managing Successfully Across Cultures.* Sonoma, California: Nicholas Brealey Publishers, 1996.

Lind, Michael. 'To have and have not.' *Harpur's* June 1995:35. Retrieved October 10, 2000 from Bell & Howell database (ProQuest Direct) on the World Wide Web: *http://proquest.umi.com*

Linn, Linda. *Landing Your First Real Job.* New York: McGraw Hill, 1996.

Lipsky, David & Abrams, Alexander. *Late Bloomers.* New York: Times Books, 1994.

McDonough, Patricia M. *Choosing Colleges.* Albany: State University of New York, 1997.

McMenamin, Brigid. 'The tyranny of the diploma.' *Forbes* 28 December 1998: 104.

McRae, Hamish. *The World in 2020.* Cambridge, Mass.: Harvard Business School Press, 1994.

Michael, Robert T., et al. *Sex in America.* Boston: Little, Brown, 1994.

Occupational Outlook Handbook. United States Labor Department, 1996–97.

Sauve, Roger. *Borderlines.* Toronto & Montreal: McGraw-Hill Ryerson, 1994.

Soros, George. 'The capitalist threat.' *Atlantic Monthly* February 1997: 45.

Stanley, Thomas J. *The Millionaire Mind*. Kansas City: Andrew McMeel Publishing, 2000.

Strauss, William & Howe, Neil. *The Fourth Turning*. New York: Broadway Books, 1997. *Generations*. New York: Morrow and Company, 1991.

'A Survey of Canada.' *The Economist* 24 July 1999.

Terrenzini & Pascarellaf. *How College Affects Students*. San Francisco: Jossey Bass, 1991.

Thurow, Lester. *Head to Head: The Coming Economic Battle Among Japan, Europe, and America*. New York: Warner Books, 1992.

Tyler, John, et al. 'Are more college graduates really taking 'high school' jobs.' *Monthly Labor Review* December 1995: 18.

'The way we work now.' *New York Times Magazine* March 5, 2000.

Wegmann, Robert G. *Work in the New Economy*. Alexandria, VA: American Association for Counseling and Development, 1989.